MW01097605

COOLPOSING

Jesse,

Thanks for the support and keep up the good work.

— Dr. George Cross

COOLPOSING

Secrets of Black Male
Leadership in America

Dr. George Cross, DM

Library of Congress Control Number: 2010915152
ISBN: Hardcover   978-1-4535-9544-2
                   Softcover   978-1-4535-9543-5
                   Ebook   978-1-4535-9545-9

To order additional copies of this book, contact:
Xlibris Corporation
1-888-795-4274
www.Xlibris.com
Orders@Xlibris.com
87340

CONTENTS

"No race, no ethnic group, has suffered so much over so long a span as Blacks have, and do still, at the hands of those who benefited from the connivance of the United States government, from slavery and the century of legalized American racial hostility that followed it [including lynching]. It is a miracle that the victims-weary dark souls long shorn of a venerable and ancient identity-have survived at all, stymied as they are by the blocked roads to economic equality"

[Randall Robinson, *The Debt*]

This book is about the unique and little known leadership style created by African "slaves" and their proud descendants in America, who refuse to be called "Nigga".

Birth of the Cool

In the beginning was the human rights plan for Black males. And then came the assumptions, and the assumptions were without form, and the human rights plan for Black males was completely without substance. And therefore darkness was upon the face of the people. And they spoke amongst themselves, saying, *It is a crock of doo-doo and it stinketh!*

And the people went unto their local representatives and sayeth: *It is a pail of dung and none can abide the odor thereof.*

And the Local Representatives went unto the State Representatives and sayeth: *It is a container of excrement and it is very strong such that none may abide by it.*

And the State Representatives went unto the Congresspersons and sayeth: *It is a vessel of fertilizer, and none may abide its strength.*

And the Congresspersons spoke among themselves, saying: *It contains that which aids plant growth, and it is very strong.*

And the Congress went unto the Senate and sayeth: *It promotes growth and is very powerful.*

And the Senate went unto the President and sayeth: *This new human rights plan for Black males will actively promote growth and efficiency of America.*

And finally, the President looked upon the human rights plan for Black males and saw that it was good, and the Human Rights Plan became the Policy of how Black males in America will be mistreated and overlooked as leaders.

In a direct response to being disrespected, and violated, Black males chose to become "Cool", which led to *Coolposing*.

PREFACE

My experience at University of Phoenix stretched my imagination to incredible dimensions from which it could never return to its previous limited capacity. I encountered theories which became my everyday practice and ultimately transformed my thinking to "scholar-practitioner." I now am known as one of the deepest thinking educators throughout my school district and am included in projects, committees, or panels that bring together the district leaders.

As a doctoral learner, I witnessed a remarkable occurrence. I was not as prepared for the coursework as I thought I was, however, the faculty members, such as Dr. Lloyd C. Williams and Dr. Marilyn K. Simon seemed to be aware of this fact in advance. The courses moved at a pace of what famed child psychologist Lev Vygotsky refers to as "the zone of proximal development." This is the area that is just beyond the grasp, which motivates the learner to reach for in earnest, while the teacher skillfully moves the goal further away, but appropriately so. This gentle dance of scholarship, with the learner reaching and the teacher beckoning, guided me through the Coolposing research process without me ever feeling that the goal was permanently beyond my reach.

The event that made me fully appreciate my University of Phoenix education was the commencement ceremony when I was awarded my doctorate. I was unable to make it to the ceremony attended by most doctoral learners, so I participated in the ceremony at the University of Phoenix campus near me. I was the only graduate being awarded a doctorate, which permitted me to lead in the contingent of 325 graduates. The feeling of walking into the auditorium first, as the leader, sent chills through me. Then being the first name called, recognized as a doctor, then hooded in front of hundreds of wildly applauding people who did not know me until that moment, was telling. They were applauding the achievement. I stood there fighting back the tears as the applause continued for what seemed like an eternity. I was transformed in that moment. I became Dr. George Cross, III, America's foremost scholar of Coolposing leadership.

ACKNOWLEDGEMENT

For my wife, Debbie, and all my children,
In celebration of the treasures that defy language.

My mother, Josephine Cross and father, George M. Cross, Jr.

My sisters, Faith, Loretta, Marvella, Francine, Cherise,
and brother, Vernon

My doctoral dissertation committee-Lloyd C. Williams, D. Min., Ph.D.;
Marilyn K. Simon, Ph.D.; and A. S. Mahdi Ibn-Ziyad, Ph.D.

My students, administrators and teachers in the Camden City Schools
and Philadelphia School District

My colleagues at Rowan University, University of Pennsylvania, and
University of Phoenix

QUOTES FROM COOLPOSING

"I have become meaner and more cynical. The job has made me hard for my protection. The 'tough guy' look is part of my way of controlling things."

"I express myself calmly related to disrespect, but I always have the knowledge of how to disguise my anger."

"Being cool is very different from staying cool. Anybody can be cool for a little while . . . the trick is to maintain your cool."

"Slickness is my way of being cool and hip at the same time; it's my way of being legitimate, while I have fun."

"I was looked on as cool because of the way I dressed and used the latest slang."

"I flow with the tide; I made friends with the African-type groups, you know, the 'way out' types, and looked at African art a lot."

"Those rich fat cats downtown control everything. I don't have to say any names; you know who I mean. Well, they can't control my manhood and my confidence; that's what I have when I stay cool. Nobody can ever take that from me. Nobody!"

INTRODUCTION

The experience of writing this book involved a frightening reality: Dr. Cross had to abandon much of his caution and security and run blindly through unchartered territory, secretly feeling that he would come out all right. This intentionally confusing and *Coolposing* act is precisely what is mandatory for success in life. Looking back, why would he have wanted to remain who he was? He was not the commercial author of a greatly ignored yet significant scholarly subject, such as *Coolposing* so why stay that way? Since making the decision to change, he will never stop changing. He truly believes that he can either change things or make it difficult for things not to change.

Dr. Cross has presented his work on *Coolposing* in seminars and forums at conventions for state-level education associations and national conferences for Black males. He has also presented at colleges and universities, and was featured on the front page of a major newspaper in a story that showed how his work has positively affected the academic achievement of disruptive and resistant students projecting the "cool pose." In this book, his theories are placed into operational scenarios that can be applied to work places and class rooms.

Chapter 1 begins with a discussion on Black males who fear God yet still break laws in an attempt to level the unequal playing field of opportunity in America. Chapter 2 explores the concept of the negative image that surrounds Black males in America who are full of life yet are seen throughout the media as lazy. Chapter 3 examines the history and framework for why Black males keep inventing new ways to move for their survival and progress in America. Chapter 4 focuses on the long discussed issue of where Black males' rhythm comes from and it is not the jungles of Africa. Chapter 5 tackles the little known topic of why Black males B.S. so well and reveals reasons you would never have guessed. Chapter 6 provides insight into the long awaited answer of why Black males are late a whole lot and how to put an end to "CP" time. Chapter 7 puts the spotlight on gangs to discover why they matter so much to some Black males, who know their destruction in advance. Chapter 8 calls out teachers and discusses why it is up to them to better understand Black males for their and America's benefit. Chapter 9 provides actual interviews with Black males who tell when, where, how, and why they cry in many ways. Chapter 10 puts it all together with a summary of the book which identifies reasons why Black males' style cannot be copied.

This book will provide an eye opening reading experience and mark the beginning of your becoming more fully aware of the balanced and congruent human beings Black males will become through the positive use of *Coolposing* leadership.

Howard Stevenson, Ph.D., author of *Playing with Anger*

1

WHY BLACK MALES FEAR GOD YET BREAK LAWS

One of the greatest roles ever created by Western man has been the role of "Negro." One of the greatest actors to play the role has been the "Nigger."

—Henry Dumas

For a successful revolt to occur, more than cash and weapons are needed; you need a pose or philosophy-wars are founded on a point of view, or on efforts to change or totally destroy one. This book is about a pose or approach which may prove to be highly explosive to some, and even dangerous to others. It is an introduction to *Coolposing*, which is a leadership pose or philosophy based on principles linked to the West African way of life from over 5,000 years ago. *Coolposing* is a positive response by America's Black males (and *not* niggas) to alienation, lynching, and loss of community grounded in the coolness of the first group of captured, yet resistant Africans, who arrived at Jamestown, Virginia in 1619.

Coolposing proposes a major shift for the best mental, spiritual and physical health of Black males and prescribes measures for crisis intervention, as well as for preventing mental burnout. The central elements of *Coolposing* comprise nine (9) kinds of cool, which are mysticism (spiritual character), *accord* (in harmony), *flexibility* (capable to adapt), *vigor* (mental strength), *change agency* (power to make a difference), *collectivism* (group control), *communicative individuality* (sharing personality), *verboseness* (wordy), and *shared-time perspective* (moments are superior to clocks). These forces make it clear why a way of thinking of leadership that is harmonious for the stability and flexibility of Black males in America can be dynamite.

RUNNING THE *COOLPOSING* GAME

Jimmy is at his mind's end witnessing the ultimate frustration; he is a Black male who has just had his car towed and impounded and does not have enough money to retrieve it. His car is on a flatbed tow truck and it is nearing closing time. He needs the car for work and his job is outside of the public transportation zone. Every minute that ticks by shoves him further into a panic. He has no choice; he calls his close friend, Jerry, another Black male.

"Hello?"
"Jerry!"
"Jim? What's up?"
"They impounded my ride. I didn't know about the towing sign."

"Where are you?"

"I'm at Lawn Street; you know that lot there, where they . . ."

"I'm cool. Give me ten minutes; I need my suit."

"Okay, later."

Shortly after the phone conversation, a late model BMW speeds into the driveway of the impoundment station; its brakes belch loudly as the driver's door jolts open. Out jumps a tall, light complexioned Black man, dressed in a well-tailored dark blue $1,000 Armani suit, a starched white custom-fitted shirt with a silk gray $100 tie, carrying a highly polished expensive leather brief case and wearing a pair of $600 black crocodile-skinned cap toe business shoes. *"Put that car down!"* he barks without looking at anyone in particular but pointing and shouting loud enough that everyone responds. He quickly flashes his badge and continues shouting orders, *"I want the names of everybody who works here-especially the owner. You have thirty seconds to release that car!"* He hits the speed-dial button on his cell phone, *"Yeah, I'm here. It's just what I thought. Don't send the squad, I got this. I'll call you back!"*

He checks his watch with an attitude, defiantly eyes the tow truck operator, and quickly walks toward Jimmy, *"It's under control. You sounded like it was deeper than it is, so I called the squad. I'll call 'em back in a few to tell 'em it's lightweight."* The tow truck operator reluctantly moves toward the truck. *"Hurry up, you got ten seconds!"* Jerry shouts. The operator speeds up. He lowers the car off the flatbed and Jerry maintains devastating eye contact with everyone at the station. *"I'll have to charge him $25 for one day's impoundment,"* the owner says timidly. *"He ain't paying a damn cent!"* Jerry roars back, keeping his piercing eyes directly on the owner. The owner freezes, with no come back.

Jimmy snatches the keys from the tow truck operator once the car is safely down, and enters the car cautiously, as Jerry chimes in, *"Jim, check it out. Look for any scratches or dents you see that were not there before; these cats are good for messing up people's rides."* Jimmy quickly looks the car over, seeing no damage he slides into the seat and starts it up. Jerry gives him the signal to wait, and hits speed-dial again, *"Lieutenant Cromarty? Jerry; it's cool. Look, I'll need a car to patrol this area tomorrow; know what I mean? Okay. Cool."*

Jerry gives the "go" sign, and Jimmy slowly backs out, as Jerry strolls gangster-like toward his BMW. The tow truck operator, the other drivers and the owner grimly watch as Jerry climbs in, yells to Jimmy, *"Follow me!"* and screeches away. Five blocks later, Jerry pulls over, with Jimmy close behind, they get out, give each other a "high five", and a smiling Jerry says to Jimmy, *"It works every time, my brother!"*

Was the action legitimate? Here is what just took place: Jerry is neither a police detective nor a patrolman; he is a security officer working in a public school system that simply put on his Sunday best to help a friend. Jimmy called Jerry because he knew that the worst that could happen was their scheme was exposed and he would just end up paying for the towing and impoundment fees that he rightfully owed. Jimmy and Jerry, who both fear God yet broke the law, are classic examples of those who understand the need to put up a *front*, and they know how powerful and rewarding keeping up a front can be. Fronting is the foundation of Coolposing.

Keeping up their fronts is the major concern of most groups; Black, White, rich, poor, male, female, young, old, gay, straight, high academic achievers, special needs students, hip-hop musicians, symphony orchestra members, law abiding citizens and career criminals alike. Nearly everybody wants to keep up a front-especially in America, which is considered by many to be the unofficial fronting capital of the universe. The group that has arguably kept up its front with the most style, urgency, desperation and passion-for the longest time-is Black males, which is why they are the focus of this book. The brief history of fronting that follows helps simplify why Black males hold their fronts even in the face of great danger.

When slave auctioneers had exceptional merchandise, they sold it separately. When they found the "items" flawed in some way-age, illnesses, deformities, etc.-they sold them in lots, frequently of a dozen. Every slave knew that he was included among a dozen only if something was physically wrong with him. Thus, to be a part of a dozen was humiliating.

Eventually, the term "dozens" applied to a verbal battle that black people developed to insult and humiliate each other. The focus was on genealogy and the point was total humiliation. Yet, the loser was the one who, because his emotions took control or because his insults were too weak, took refuge in physical abuse.

The winner was the one with the cruelest wit who managed to keep cool.

—The Black Book

Over four hundred years through the founding of Jamestown, Virginia, the signing of the Declaration of Independence and the US Constitution, the ratification of the Emancipation Proclamation, and rollbacks of gains made by Blacks through the Civil Rights struggle, insists that positive public images of Black males do not exist. Black males have a lot to say, however that begins by controlling their own images, which has never truly happened in America. Although the myth of Black males in business for themselves being inferior to others in countless ways never really *was*, the myth always somehow *is*, primarily for lack of control of their desired public image.

The *coolposing* game is necessary to master as a Black male businessman in America, the country, which has an unflattering history of preying upon and damaging the images of members of groups such as Native Americans, Asian Americans, Latinos, and Blacks. The forefathers conceived, implemented and enforced the laws and rules that govern business without any input of nonwhite citizens. The *coolposing* game is the equalizer, which levels the playing field for those shut out of the power. The following is how a Black male music promoter shares his view of coolposing performances:

Being detached from the troublemakers prevents problems. That is the key to survival. That is how I do it. I overcome discrimination and other problems with slickness. When someone is harassing me, I can choose to get violent, ignorant or use some other aggressive behavior . . . but either way I lose. If I get arrested for hurting someone, even if I am right, my business suffers. If I blow my cool, I lose my reputation and my ability to make a living. That's why I have to be slick. Slickness is being legitimate and hip at the same time. It's a way of being cool that requires skillful maneuvering to contribute to my business.

The music producer provides a sound reason for behavior that may be faked and less than professional, however it is precisely how the *coolposing* game is played. His detachment from others is the front that allows him to remain calm in crises and gives him the advantage over those attempting to distract him through shaky business practices, such as inaccurate accounting, false claims, racism, and forged documents. The music producer maintains a front, or a mask that he chooses the world to see, which enables him to succeed in his desired role. The *front* is a necessary strategy for many Black males in business who agree that these desperate times require equally desperate measures.

FRONTING

A new student reports to a highly regarded Ivy League university in the northeast. "Hello, sir, I was told there would be a counselor to see me about financial aid sometime this morning". The puzzled professor looks at the unfamiliar student and says, "No one told me anything about it." The student begins to name drop, "Dr. Portnoy and I met and she told me Professor Stevenson wanted me to register for this class, even though I missed the deadline, because of the work I did at my previous school". Both of the names carry much weight and prestige at the university, therefore the professor, not willing to risk going against them says, "Well, okay then, take a seat, sign the attendance sheet, and we can settle the financial issue when the counselor arrives". The counselor never shows up, the student sits in on a free Ivy League class, and has laid the possible groundwork for a tuition-free course.

A person's identity is attached to the front that he or she chooses to keep up. It offers a false picture of his or her self to the world. The goal of fronting is to actually morph into the desired role that is played by dressing the part, changing the walking and talking style, traveling in the appropriate circle of friends and associates, and in some cases, it even requires embracing the necessary religion. Society's lack of caution provides a whole lot of evidence that fronting accomplishes its goals more frequently than not. Successful fronting deceives others by the concept of *fake it 'til you make it*, proving Abraham Lincoln essentially wrong: You *can* indeed fool all the people, all the time (or so many of them that it seems like all of them).

How many times have you entered a restaurant, bank, agency, or store and attempted to guess who the person in charge was, and discovered you were wrong? Did you believe the person wearing the most expensive shoes was in charge? What about the person wearing the darkest suit? How about the person who talked the most? Probably, there were many times you thought you knew who the leader was and you were dead wrong. This is a reality in America, because it is so easy to put up a front that takes a while for others to discover. More people than you could imagine are not who they made you believe they really were.

National news programs are frequently bursting with stories of prominent athletic coaches, or government officials nominated for cabinet level posts that were forced to resign in disgrace because they falsified their credentials on resumes and applications. These coaches and officials never thought that the only thing authorities had to do was pick up the phone and check with the college or university from which they claimed to have received a degree. It probably never entered their minds because they played their roles so long and so well that they were just as deceived by their performances as their audiences (it is called *hubris*).

Fronting produces an agreed upon, though deceptive reality, coined by Richard Majors, Ph.D., as "cool pose". Cool pose is a riddle whose confusing answer usually involves a pun that never truly provides a straight answer, such as "What came first, the chicken or the egg?" The brilliance in cool pose is that it rejoices in its own mysteriousness. Those who possess coolness intentionally hide their nature with slick words and fake performances.

The creation of more humorous uses of words to suggest dozens of its meanings or the meaning of a word similar in sound is the mission of those displaying coolness, such as "I heard you twice the *first* time," "It's about to get ugly *all up* in here," and "Well shut my mouth wide *open*!" Of course there is no possible way one could hear something "twice" when it was only spoken once; there is no way something can occur "all up" anywhere, and a shut mouth cannot at the same time be "wide open", yet coolness makes all of these things so. The significance of coolness is that its mystical past foretold and is ceaselessly foretelling its unknowable future.

Coolness for Black males is the lived experience of coping with a life of insignificance. The United States permits half of its Black men to be unemployed, stands by idly as schools turn promising Black children into failures, and too often allows the abuse of Blacks by police or their group exploitation by evil realtors, insurance salespersons and merchants to go unpunished. Coolness is the mask to hide some Black males' despair of these type injustices while providing a cool front of masculinity that is crucial for the preservation of pride, dignity, and respect. Few social or mental creations shape, direct, or control Black males as strongly as coolness does.

"Yeah, you think you so bad. You mess around and get in my face and I will put an ass-kicking on you that will have you more broken than the 10 Commandments!" shouts a Black male at his rival. The reality is the threat is being made out of pure fear; he had not been in a serious fight in his entire life. His threat has to be so outlandish that even if the rival is a more experienced fighter, he will have to at least consider the remote chance that the shouter could deliver on the threat, and as a result, calm himself down.

Coolness provides survival for some Black males to expressively detach from the constant strain of an unfriendly and often deadly society. Perceived reality is the belief in an exacting role, which prompts some Black men to assume the role of coolness for superiority, self-respect and honor. This helps them accept the fact that they are losing ground to others, in academics, politics, business and leadership, not through their lack of effort, yet through discrimination coupled with shrewdly carried out and well-funded schemes and nasty lies against them. Lying on a Black male is nearly a spectator sport now, with so many people, including school children, participating in the scheme. It is almost a rare sighting to see a Black male teacher in public schools because of the fear of being accused of something outrageous, yet believed.

LIES AGAINST BLACK MALES

"I was just sitting in my car, minding my own business and two Black men stuck a gun in my face and robbed me of $500. I was scared to death, so I just handed it over" claims a well dressed White man. Police ask for a description and begin rounding up the usual suspects-Black males. After further investigation it is discovered that the White male actually lost the money gambling at the casino and could not face his awaiting angry wife, so he concocted a high percentage story that could have kept him out of trouble.

Black males are in the forefront of coolness for no other reason than their ability to consistently outsmart the racist system they have found themselves stuck in since their first group presence in Jamestown, Virginia in 1619. They are the ideal actors, not just in America, but globally. Much of Black males' acting comes from their need to react to falsehoods made up worldwide so that others can keep their phony advantages, entitlement, and sense of power politically, socially, legally, economically, and educationally. Even Shakespeare's *Othello*, the fictional Black Moor and namesake of the play, was lied on by White *Iago* in Act I, Scene I: "I am one, sir that comes to tell you your daughter and the Moor are making the beast with two backs". This claim of filthy lovemaking to *Desdemona's* father is the lie that destroys *Othello*.

A cycle of lies against Black males has forced them to sharpen their skills of managing their cool under great crisis. A White man (Charles Stewart) killed his wife in Massachusetts, created a lie and staged a crime scene that appeared to clear him, then he claimed it was a Black man that did it, and area police rounded up nearly every Black man breathing. A White woman (Susan Smith) in South Carolina drowned her two small boys in a sunken car, appeared on national television shaken and tearful, then claimed a Black man did it, and police again rounded up every Black man in sight.

Strong evidence eventually exposed Stewart and Smith as guilty and both faced the consequences of their crimes: Stewart committed suicide and the state convicted Smith of murder. The trend of Whites lying on Black men to escape justice has existed since slavery; in fact, some Black males feel they need not apply to acting school for dramatic skills, it would only waste their time and money-American life has made them the greatest role players in this nation's history.

We wear the mask that grins and lies
It hides our cheeks and shades our eyes,-
This debt we pay to human guile;
With torn and bleeding hearts we smile,
And mouth with myriad subtleties.

Why should the world be overwise,
In counting all our tears and sighs?
Nay let them only see us, while
We wear the mask.

We smile, but, O great Christ, our cries
To thee from tortured souls arise
We sing, but oh the clay is vile
Beneath our feet, and long the mile;
But let the world dream otherwise,
We wear the mask!

—Paul Laurence Dunbar

"All the world's a stage and all the men and women merely players. They have their exits and their entrances, and one man in his time plays many parts"—William Shakespeare. This well known observation by Shakespeare is the summary of the Black male's existence. The essence of coolness is alive in every award winning performance by Black males, such as Jimmy and Jerry, who craftily retrieved a legally towed and impounded vehicle with limited control or access to power or resources. They showed coolness: *We are as intelligent as those who are distressing us even though they have more authority and resources than we do.* The vitality of coolness, with its unlimited potential for constructing fantastic scenarios, psychologically empowers the Black male and safely hides his identity, just as an armored mask would.

HOW COOLNESS WORKS

Imagine this scene: Matt, who is a Black male, wearing an $800 suit, $300 shoes, $100 shirt, and $80 necktie, enters a fancy predominately White restaurant, smiles, is cool, and shakes hands with the manager, then confidently seats himself in a section marked "reserved". The waiters look at him, look back at each other, and quickly glance at the manager as if to ask, "Who the hell is this Negro?" Matt reads the menu and immediately summons a waiter and asks, "Have the others arrived or called yet? I am early because I have a flight to the coast later. Can I order now?"

The confused manager, who has no one else to ask, and has no guest list for the reserved section, pretends to know him, which maintains his front of being in control, then instructs a waiter to take his order, fearing that not to do so may anger the others in the reserved party when they arrive. Matt orders from the top of the menu, eats well alone, pays his bill, and leaves. None of the others ever arrive in the reserved section. What happened?

In reality, Matt is a local street hustler who simply wanted a decent meal with a nice view, which he could afford, yet was not well connected enough to enjoy it in the exclusive restaurant. He called ahead and made a phony reservation for an important sounding organization-"The Germantown-Mt. Airy Jaycees". He set the reservation time an hour later than he arrived, which gave him the luxury of coolposing with no chance of being caught.

Image control, or the ability to project the needed or desired look, which is what coolness really is, shows phony feelings to others through inversion or "upside-downness", which reverses the position, order, form and relationship of real behaviors and desired impressions. The skillful management of deceit can turn situations between the performer and the audience inside out or upside down. Ultimately, the inversion or upside-downness, produce behavior where *bad* means "good" and *wicked* means "spectacular". The mystic or cool behavior fills persons with spiritual insight, enlightenment and glorification as they gain powerful advantages over others fooled by the performance of their "game". Many of these games are so well-played and skillfully operated that those fooled by the maneuvers describe the players in terms such as "deft", "slick", "righteous" and "smooth", which are synonyms for cool.

Coolness, gaming, slicking, conning, and hustling were once considered negative approaches to relationships in the traditionally dishonest workplace of the depression era 1920s and 1930s. During this period, bosses would make promises of higher wages to factory workers and laborers which were rarely fulfilled, and their excuses were followed with more unfulfilled promises, while the workers remained silent. If they complained at all they risked a fist in the mouth or a club across the back of the head, since there were no unions at that time.

Today's world feels people need to express their negative emotions as well as the positive ones to provide a balanced and honest representation of them selves. It is not hard to see why many are upset with cool individuals who are thought to convey dishonesty by the outward and purposeful suppression of their negative emotions through fronting. Cool is viewed as phony to many however the coolest individuals in many groups usually end up on top (think about boxing promoters and rap music record producers and owners).

"Good morning. My, that is a beautiful suit you are wearing. Are you Mr. Jones, interviewing for the position of Help Desk Manager?" The receptionist says all the right words to set a wonderful tone for the job interview. At the conclusion of the interview she adds, "You did very well. You should be hearing from our Human Resources Department shortly. Do not call us." That is the last he will hear from that company.

How many times have you been greeted at a job interview by a smiling receptionist who falsely raised your hopes, while she knew all the while that you would not be hired because the job was promised to someone else and the interview was just a legal requirement? Or she just did not like you personally. Unexpressed negative emotions tell others that one is hateful by using responses that expose his or her insincerity.

A major part of the 1960s message was the revolt against coolness and the suppression of feelings. Many were being genuine, spontaneous, and free in expressing their sincere feelings in social events or happenings such as *Woodstock*, communal living, love children, the Civil Rights Movement and the idea of giving peace a chance. The actions of the so-called *flower children* of the 1960s attempted to show the world that unlike the mind, the heart found it difficult to lie.

Too many poor young Black males rob stores, people, and banks to get money so they can give themselves an extreme makeover that they believe will give them a new life. Unfortunately, they overlook important things like better education, greater involvement in people, enhanced vocabulary, and more love in their hearts as key ways to make themselves over. Therefore, the males become poorer because even with the ill-gotten money, they are eventually caught as they make mistakes such as park the stolen Mercedes in a low rent district project tenement, wear gaudy clothing to a neighborhood bar, or try to break a $100 bill at a neighborhood candy store. They are trapped in their ignorance and their criminal behavior qualifies them for scholarships to *clown college*.

Image control is actually a sincere accomplishment for the purposes of its users and it earns respect from others that value the detached style as a form of coolness, especially in ghettoes and diverse inner city communities. Coolness stabilizes and minimizes threatening situations for many by providing an inner strength that remarkably improves the player's confidence. The 1800s Black males, who were either on the slave plantation or working in a sharecropper, or powerless position, were threatened with violence if they were seen to desire independence by earning a living outside of their set role of plantation hand. To avoid detection and hostility, the Black males who sought independence, exercised a disciplined self-restraint that masked their intentions and took the form of coolness. Some enslaved Black males were actually the coolest; under the cruelest circumstances, they exercised the customary Black American motto describing cleverness, which is *"every closed eye ain't sleep and every goodbye ain't gone"*.

The closer one comes to danger; more brightly do the ways into the saving power begin to shine [Where danger is, coolness provides the saving power]

—Martin Heidegger

Within coolness, which will be further developed in this book as a central element for emerging leadership strategies for Black males, exists the courage to be daring, yet cunning in order to survive a fierce attack with the fewest possible casualties. Observe the following account of coolness as a hidden strategy:

The CEO of a major corporation had taken ill and was lying on his hospital bed very close to death. He summoned his most reliable and trustworthy employee of 20 years to make a deathbed confession:

"Johnson, you know I have counted on your undying loyalty for the past two decades."
"Yes, sir."
"And you never let me down."
Yes, sir."
"Well, Johnson, it seems I have not been totally honest with you."
"Yes, sir."

27

"I held back many raises from you, for fear of losing you to another department."

"Yes, sir."

"I also forged your signature to steal benefits from you."

"Yes, sir."

"And Johnson, I also slept with your wife." "Yes, sir."

"Well, Johnson, my conscience is clear now so I can die in peace. By the way Johnson, do you have anything to say about what I just told you?"

"Yes, sir, that is why I poisoned you!"

The scenario shows that no matter how badly Johnson, the faithful employee, had been treated, and no matter how much the dying CEO did to keep him deprived of the necessary resources for him to advance, such as withholding raises and stealing from him, through sheer coolness, Johnson got the ultimate upper hand, which is winning the final advantage over his oppressor.

COOLNESS IN CORPORATE AMERICA

A Black male begins work at a highly regarded corporation and reports to the supervisor for his assignment.

"Hi, I'm John, a new hire, and I was told you would show me my assignment". "Certainly, John, welcome aboard".

"Will I get a chance to use my degree here?"

"What is your degree in?"

"Real Estate Management."

"Great. You are familiar with taking care of property and land."

"Yes sir, I sure am."

"Okay, here's a broom and a mop; sweep up this part of the *property*, then mop that part of the *land*."

Nobody tells all he or she knows, and this holds true as the base for fronting in the workplace. Key corporations function through deception by maneuvering around issues involving sincerity and truthful working relationships. Some executives are careful on all subjects requiring honesty, and choose a deceitful management style that allows them to talk loud and say nothing. *The Temptations*, a popular *Motown* rhythm and blues singing group, examined this deceitful management style in their lyrics: "Smiling faces, sometimes tell lies."

The collapse of the Enron Corporation ranks as the worse case of deceptive management in the history of America; all because thousands of employees, now destroyed financially, trusted the executives' smiling faces. At the top of the skillful fraud behind Enron was Kenneth Lay, a frequent dinner guest at the White House who was on a first name basis with former President George W. Bush-Bush called him "Kenny Boy". Lay was accused in a federal indictment of participating in a conspiracy to manipulate Enron's quarterly financial results, making public statements about Enron's financial performance that were false and misleading, and omitting facts necessary to make financial statements accurate and fair. The Securities and Exchange Commission filed civil charges against Lay, accusing him of fraud and insider trading and seeking recovery of more than $90 million in what the agency said were illegal proceeds from stock sales.

Enron's CEO was an insider and those duped by his massive deception through coolness and detachment, were outsiders. Enron's collapse in late 2001 cost investors billions of dollars; put thousands of Enron employees out of work and wiped out retirement savings for many. Lay, who died shortly afterward of a heart attack, chose to conceal, distort and mislead shareholders and employees whom he owed a duty of complete truthfulness. Being cool might have saved some of the vanquished employees by providing them a keener insight into outsmarting the insiders, by first of all, not believing them.

The CBS investigative reporting show, *"60 Minutes"* reveal feature after feature of White landlords refusing to rent or lease to Black tenants under the guise of excuses such as "The apartment is occupied now," or "Your application was not received in time," while a White applicant comes moments later and secures the same apartment. The ABC investigative reporting show, *"Nightline"* has made it a tradition to have a commentator skillfully interview a White employer until he or she breaks under pressure and blurts out, "Yes, the Black employees are paid less, hired last and fired first!" National restaurant franchises, *Denny's, Cracker Barrel, Red Lobster, TGIF Fridays,* and many others have admitted guilt in using subversive methods to mistreat Blacks. A Black male photographer with over 25 years experience as a businessman of his own photo studio shares his experience with unfair business treatment:

I mask my fear of the uncertainty of business with a necessary front to provide balance; I was always a hustler and I used self-esteem to manipulate customers that tended to complain. I couldn't give money back, like larger businesses-I'd go broke. I had to lie. Customers often view White males as smarter or better and workers tend to not give me as much effort as they would to White males. I know unskilled Whites who could get loans easily while loans were difficult for me and many other Black males to get-and we were better photographers. I realized early that "brothers" got messed over by the banks.

Employment of inner city Blacks and Latinos drops significantly without some degree of strong government commitment to fair hiring practices such as Office of Equal Opportunity. People of color found, with the level of their skills aside, Whites on the average received recommendations for the best jobs and occupational slots in the economy (not to mention better service at *Denny's*). Insincere managers were responsible for ushering in institutionalized distortion of the truth regarding Black and Latino employment equity that led to decades of economic gaps. A study by a Columbia University professor, as reported by various national news services found that in New York City, a White male with a criminal record was hired faster than a Black male who has never acted against the law. Much of the deception seen in today's employment and service areas is a continuum of American racist policy makers and businessmen from centuries ago, who have been in cohort to maintain the image of the Black male as a dangerous criminal.

We nurse their young and clean their homes
They laugh at us and give us bones
We work their fields in blazing sun
They under pay us when we're done.

—Frederick Douglass (1853)

The irony of the mostly impoverished Black male being projected as a constant criminal while mostly wealthy others continue to steal billions is ridiculous. It is obvious that Black males in America could never steal as much as White males because the opportunity does not, and will never exist. White males have access to billions of dollars, which they steal regularly, yet continue to shine the spotlight on Black males as they steal miniscule amounts in comparison. Wall Street trader, Michael Milken stole so much money that he paid a $600 million fine and went to a country club jail as a hero with so many people gathered to view his entry that police barricades were needed to hold them back.

Black males adopt coolposing characteristics in order to not lose their cool, while they think about people such as Milken, who is a thief beyond belief, however he is a member of the Wall Street billionaire club. Members of this exclusive club seem to be made into lesser thieves by some hidden rule of the wealthy class, which determine the hidden rules of the middle class, and instruct them to never tell the lower classes about these rules. Unfortunately, the lower class is imprisoned and held accountable for every hidden rule of the wealthy and middle class that they violate, while never truly understanding why.

> It is not my job to run this train,
> Its whistle I can't blow;
> It's not my job to drive this train,
> Or take it fast or slow;
> It's not my job to steer this train,
> Or even ring the bell;
> But let this damn thing jump the track,
> And see who catches hell!

The detachment of emotion and the refusal to become enraged over injustice after injustice is recognized in the irony of the poem. All of the responsibilities of managing the train in the poem are withheld from the speaker, yet the speaker has the full blame placed in his lap when things do not go well. That train is the "American Railroad" which has been running since 1776, has carried passengers who came in huddled masses yearning to be free yet still denies Black males equal access. Coolposing is one of the most effective responses to the national attempt to brand Black males as "zeroes" instead of heroes, while overlooking the wonder of their group accomplishments as the Massachusetts 54th (first all black company of civil war soldiers), Tuskegee Airmen (first all black flying group), Black WW II Navy Veterans (first group of black sailors), Buffalo Soldiers, Red Ball Express (all black Army supply unit), and in a distorted and sick manner, the Tuskegee 626 Syphilis experiment subjects (Black men used as guinea pigs). Essentially, the refusal to stand by silently and allow further abuse to the psyche resulted in the development of coolposing behaviors which created the restorative maneuvers that provide Black males with "protection" from further hurt, harm, and danger to their minds.

2

WHY BLACK MALES ARE FULL OF LIFE YET ARE SEEN AS LAZY

We make soul with our behavior, for soul does not come already made in heaven [or paradise]. *It is only imagined there; an unfulfilled project trying to grow down.*

—James Hillman

Getting a job is perhaps the most frightening event for a recent high school graduate from an inner city high school widely known by all, as an unofficial "dumping ground." These schools are often occupied by students that have negatively exited traditional or comprehensive learning facilities because of severe rule infractions such as fighting, disrespecting authority, chronic disruption or extreme truancy. The curriculums of these "alternative schools" are often devoid of academically challenging material and consist essentially of busy work of the most elementary nature. Students assigned to these facilities rarely graduate nor do they successfully transition back to their sending schools; they usually drop out. Some of them make out even worse; they are *given* a diploma. The first serious interview too frequently occurs in the following manner:

"Next!"

"Uh, afternoon, I'm um, here for a job."

"What can you do?"

"I can do anything."

"I am not looking for someone who 'can do anything'. What are your skills?"

"I can run pretty fast. We placed second in the Penn Relays in the quarter mile relay."

"That's nice. Why didn't you apply for a track scholarship?"

"I was going to, but I filled out the papers too late. I have to wait a year."

"Oh, too bad. Now, what other skills do you have?"

"I can spell pretty good."

"No good. We have 'spell check' on all of our computers. What else can you do?"

"Ah, uh, well, I have a high school diploma."

"Look, everybody here better have a high school diploma. What other skills?"

"Um . . ."

"Look son, tell me the truth. Did you graduate, or were you socially promoted?"

"I graduated. I marched down the aisle with a cap and gown, and I . . ."

"How many credits did you earn?"

"Let's see . . . 20 in woodshop, 15 in cosmetology, 10 in daycare, 10 in art, 5 in . . ."

"Wait! What did you learn? You need 110 credits to graduate, right?"

"Yes."

"You just named over half of the required credits, and none are usable here!"

"My counselor told me . . ."

"I can't help what your counselor told you. We can't use you for this job."

"But, I have a high school diploma. I was told the diploma would be my ticket"

"Oh, it's your ticket all right . . . YOUR TICKET TO NOWHERE!"

Picture a Black man, of nearly thirty
Wearing clothes that are old, torn and dirty
Give him a job shining shoes
Or cleaning toilets with bus station crews
Give him six children with nothing to eat
And expose them to life on a ghetto street
Tie an old rag around his wife's head
And have her pregnant and lying in bed
Then stuff then all into a Northern house
And tell them once again how bad things are down South

—Gil Scott-Heron

As the academic picture becomes bleak for Black and Latino students, and the so-called achievement gap widens between them and their White and Asian American counterpart, economics begins to play a larger role in understanding why the gap remains. The school achievement gap, which is really an Education Gap or Opportunity Gap, is not about school at all but in the broader context of how children grow up. The achievement gap's roots lie well beyond the reach of schools; it is a matter of culture. Culture is defined simply as *the way we do things around here*, and jobs and employment of Blacks has to be done other than the way it was usually done-working for others.

To begin to focus on the new leadership strategies for Black males advocated in this book, there must be a clear understanding of the gains through experimentation.

There is no accepted leadership style, strategy or process tailored specifically for the equality of Black males, grounded in African cultural-based values. Cool, through a jazz viewpoint, which is *"Coolposing"*, can take a great step in that direction. One of the most significant tests of leadership is the management of one's own business enterprise. The following overview of Black business sets the proper stage to bring leadership coolness with jazz influence or *"Coolposing"*, into completion.

BLACK MALE SELF-EMPLOYMENT HISTORY

"Yo, Rob, can you drive a tow truck?"
"Yeah. I have one that runs okay"
"You want a job?"
"Yeah. What's it pay?"
"You get half the amount of every car that you tow. Each tow is $100."
"Cool. That's $50 for each car."
"Oh. I forgot. You need to pay out another $10 for my commission fee."
"Um, that cuts it down to $40."
"Well, actually $30; there's a $10 tax for each tow-that's 10% of the $100."
"I don't know. It is hard to make it on $30 a tow."
"Think about it; right now you are not making anything."
"But it's my tow truck!"
"Yeah, and it's my towing business."
"Well, all right, then . . . but $30?"

To offset education discrimination, which nearly eliminated them from professional employment consideration, Black male self-employment was constant from 1910 to 1990 at one-third the White rate; the gap was due to lower self-employment rates of Blacks in all industries. Whites and others relied more often than Blacks did on their own resources (such as networks of kinship, friendship and community ties), which are instrumental in establishing and operating their businesses. Black businessmen followed a less community-oriented pattern in establishing and leading their businesses. Barriers of racism with getting financing to start and manage their businesses ultimately affected Black males' business success.

The Great Black Migration, which is the movement that saw millions of Blacks leave the south and move north for jobs and opportunities, had no large effects on the racial self-employment gap. There was expected to be a racial balance in self-employment rates over time however it did not happen because of continuing *factors* reducing Black male self-employment. Research indicates that issues of institutional discrimination were the key reasons for some of the limited Black participation in self-employment.

Lack of exposure to business was a main source for fewer Black male businessmen; in addition the absence of Black run businesses in Black neighborhoods did not encourage businessmen. Black youths chose careers that were open as opposed to those they would prefer and as a result, fewer Black males considered business careers because being a visible minority appeared to hurt the Black community in starting and operating businesses. Black male businessmen relied on decision-making and leadership styles, which were often lacking professional education and support of fellow businessmen to counter discrimination when looking for suitable premises to rent, lease or purchase.

Blacks located their businesses outside of the segregated ethnic areas, created through racial exclusion and discrimination, which prevented minority merchants from exercising their location choice. Segregated protected markets did not appear to provide the advantages to Black businessmen that were originally imagined. Black businesses fueled by risk-taking leadership conducting business outside the ghetto's protected market consistently outperformed their counterparts doing business within it. In other words, it appeared that Whites and others trusted Black merchants more often when they were not operating in Black neighborhoods. This suggests that moving a Black business out of the ghetto area reduced the imagined danger felt by outsiders coming in to make purchases, and it indicates that Black businesses do better when not depending only on Black customers.

Among 359 Black executives surveyed, 45% believed racial prejudice was the most important obstacle to the further development of their careers. The nearly 400-year legacy of master-slave relationships was giving way to the rise of a sizable number of Black Americans into positions of leadership. Beginning in the early 1960s and continuing to the present, fundamental changes occurred to Blacks' ability to enter in, and move within the socioeconomic system of the United States.

The status credited to Blacks by Whites remained low and nearly 80% of the managers' responses to a racial-awareness questionnaire saw the system biased against Blacks. Cool behaviors provided some Black male businessmen the resources to scale psychological barriers in order to take advantage of opportunities, access educational and business offerings, and negotiate the mainstream of contemporary life. Black males were overwhelmingly subject to more cruel socioeconomic conditions in comparison with other groups. Some Black males used cool behaviors with more frequency and intensity than other groups to help cope with societal stress resulting from domination and bias.

COOLNESS AS A BLACK MALE COPING MECHANISM

"When I come into the Mall it seems like the store owners tell the security guards to watch me closely. I just go about my business and pay them no mind. My problem is that every time I look up, one of the guards tries to look away real fast as if he wasn't looking in the first place, and he was. I keep catching him." This is the same story told over and over again by Black males. Young and old, rich or poor, educated or uneducated, well-dressed or shabbily-dressed, it is the same story-America does not trust Black males.

Historically, Blacks have had a built-in defense system to shield them from many forms of failure, which have been a primary defense and very often an extremely realistic one. The protection system is a survival skill and a response to the economically depressed and isolated communities that developed in their environment. Playing it cool was an essential defense against further exploitation. Coolness helps to manage stress and biased situations by emphasizing the self and overcoming painful reality;

cool provides comfort and healing and helps Black males define their own roles.

Many Black males will engage in a conflict and say, "Fuck it!" which is a method of emotionally detaching from the situation and no longer feeling that the situation can cause them any further pain. Of course, they are often wrong, especially when the conflict deals with their wives, mothers of their children, children, or even their jobs. The temporary freedom felt by detaching from others for the sake of guarding against further hurt and insult often balloons into mental slavery later. They become haunted by their bad decision, and many times resort to drinking or drugs to shut the thoughts out of their minds.

In order to maintain internal balance and to protect one's self from strain, the Black male has to be cool in order to keep functioning. He has to continue to maintain a front and some kind of adaptation to the offender to preserve some social effectiveness. Opposing economic theory cannot explain why the job and economic market is not color-blind therefore despite their social status middle-class Blacks face the humiliation of race in public places that include businesses. In other words, no matter how much success the Black male finds, he cannot become non-Black.

Sociologists and political scientists found that race remained significant, even for well-off and successful Blacks that could not escape their collective identity. Acting calm, emotionless, fearless, aloof and tough, Black males strove to offset externally imposed negative images. Class is no guaranteed ticket for fair treatment so many Black males use coolness to cancel out emotional reactions of others to assess uncertain situations, such as checking into hotels that they made reservations for over the phone or standing at the car rental counter while the attendant suspiciously looks at their credit card.

The overrepresentation of Blacks in the lower class casts shadows that stereotype working- and middle-class Blacks for reasons of race alone. Black doctors, professors, engineers, administrators, teachers, and businessmen find themselves reduced to a ghetto status, more often than athletes and entertainers, based on the treatment of Whites and others in many places of business. To offset the pain, some Black males adopt *cool rules* that specify when, where and how it is culturally appropriate to express emotions, such as smiling in mostly White-patronized restaurants and enjoying the meal, despite being seated in a less than desirable section, knowing that to express their real displeasure may lead to further problems with service.

Small immigrant shop owners in inner cities rarely hire native-born Blacks, especially young males, who live nearby. The reasons they claim range from poor work attitudes of Black applicants to the lawless image of Blacks portrayed in the media. This lame excuse is given, despite the common sense that by hiring local residents, the shop's image of being a concerned neighborhood establishment would improve and business may increase. Black male's emotional self-regulation in *coolposing* adjusts their emotional state to a comfortable level in order to remain productively engaged in the surroundings.

Good name in man and woman, dear my lord,
Is the immediate jewel of their souls.
Who steals my purse steals trash.
'Tis something, nothing.
'Twas mine, 'tis his, and has been slave to thousands.
But he that filches from me my good name
Robs me of that which not enriches him
And makes me poor indeed.

—From "Othello"
William Shakespeare

EDUCATION EXPERIENCES OF BLACK MALES

"I just met this pretty and smart young lady and we are getting along well."

"What does she do?"

"Oh, I don't know. I see her coming out of the college offices a lot."

"The college offices? Fool, she is a professor in the Graduate School of Education."

"I don't care. She gave me a nice vibe."

"But you are a custodian."

"Look, man, love is deeper than numbers."

"Not numbers on paychecks, and especially when one is $30,000 more than the other."

"What? She's making that kind of paper?"

"Yes. I know, because I clean up there and I saw the pay stubs lying on her desk."

"Well, maybe I can just be her lunch date."

"Maybe."

The decline and stagnation of Black men's participation in postsecondary education caused their inability to mostly survive or to succeed in business and related fields. W. E. B. DuBois based his concern for the *talented tenth* Black male elite on his vision to make manhood the work of the schools. Ironically, the *talented tenth* has shifted from male to female as Black women, and not Black men, comprise the majority of Blacks enrolled in college receiving associate, bachelors, masters, and doctoral and professional degrees.

In 2010, Black women earned 63% of bachelor's degrees awarded to Blacks, 67% of master's degrees, 60% of doctoral degrees and 55% of professional degrees. Black women surpassed Black men in doctoral and professional degree attainment in the past 25 years. The steady decline in the American economy of low skilled, living wage jobs in which Black men with little education have historically found employment is a debilitating issue. The decline in low-skilled employment suggests Black high school students are not willingly forgoing college for greater employment opportunities. Black males complete high school at lower rates than others, which suggests that they will be blocked future access to educational opportunities by the burden of stricter entrance requirements and increased tuition.

Businesses increase with age and education level, although less known is why the expectation of increased Black educational levels fails to reduce the racial gaps in business rates. Business rates among less-educated workers and not better-educated workers over time actually reduce racial gaps. Evidence shows that trends in business ownership across educational levels are favorable to less-educated Blacks. The development of business does not carry the same demands for educational degrees as many other occupations. Traditional education of all people is important, although little known facts about the cultural context in which Black males learn and act out leadership roles, decision-making tasks and cool behavior as a coping strategy exists.

BLACK FAMILY BUSINESS EXPERIENCES

"Who's your Daddy?" is a piercing question that contains an explosive link to endless opportunities or a detour to a dead end for many Black males. The father's occupation and business connections are often the keys to opportunities for his children. A business parent makes his or her offspring two to three times likely to be a businessman as someone without a business parent. The general assumption is that business experience passes from the parents to the children. However, in spite of this theory, the lack of business experience cannot explain the low levels of Black ownership. As long as the parents were major influences, equality should have occurred reasonably quickly. The probability of the son of a self-employed man being self-employed and the son of a man not self-employed being self-employed is lower for Blacks than Whites.

Numerous factors reduce Black ownership besides the initial conditions of low Black businesses. Ongoing issues depresses the Black business rate, such as bias, skills, capital and "intangibles passed generationally", which include social, educational, economic, legal and health related issues. Among Black and White families, businesses hold disproportionately more wealth than workers do and Black businesses hold a lower fraction of Black family wealth than White businesses hold of White family wealth. Black families have a lower rate of ownership.

Black Americans have the lowest rate of self-employment and immigrant businesses are in competition with Black businesses. Scholars argue that Blacks do not possess a strong tradition of business ownership and this problem connects to not possessing networking skills important to other ethnic businesses. Black traditions in business are lacking, in large part due to slavery. Slavery disrupted the family and caused low levels of Black ownership.

There is an opposing view that shows Africans and families in American colonies, and later in the new nation, carved a meaningful history in American business. Black male businesses face struggling against having fewer role models in business than other groups and the lack of large numbers of close relatives in business when compared with Asians, Hispanics and non-minorities. Africans and family of "New World descendents" were best understood as essentially business capitalists. Evidence to challenge the stereotype that Blacks had no "business heritage" exists through Black businesspersons such as Madame C. J. Walker, the Black woman who became the *first* female millionaire, and Frederick Douglass Patterson, the first Black automaker.

There are well-documented business successes that provide significant inspiration for young Black business owners to view as role models who overcame obstacles decades ago. Due to the lack of meaningful historical records of successful Blacks in business, the stereotype of the failed businessman of color grows unchallenged. Strategies through *"Coolposing"* provide the Black male in business with African-cultural based principles that suggest stability and flexibility in organizational leadership that wipes out the failed European-based leadership style evolving from a stifling mechanistic foundation. The stiff mechanistic style is the direct opposite of the flowing organic style of leadership carried through the West African culture.

Success is counted sweetest
By those who ne'er succeed
To comprehend a nectar
Requires sorest need

Not one of all the purple host
Who took the flag today
Can tell the definition
So clear of victory

As he defeated, dying,
On whose forbidden ear
The distant strains of triumph
Burst agonized and clear

—Emily Dickinson

WAY TOO COOL FOR SCHOOL

"How was your report card?"

"I passed."

"Good. What grades did you get?"

"It doesn't really matter; I passed."

"Did you make the *Honor Roll*?"

"Hey, man, don't be talking that crap around me."

"All I said was Hon."

"Shhhh, somebody might hear."

"Like who?"

"Like my boys, stupid."

"Huh?"

"Man, if they heard me talking about that *Honor Roll* bull I'd be toast."

"I thought that was the aim of school-get as much out of it as you can."

"All I want to do is get out of it period."

"And do what?"

"Make some money."

"How? With no good education you can't make it."

"Look at the rappers. Look at the ballers. Don't tell me, man."

"Each successful rapper and baller has a one in a million story you can't relive."

"I know I'll live out my own."

"Okay, start rapping."

"I can't yet."

"Well, then start balling."

"I have to work on my game."

"Stop dreaming, and finish school."

Many inner city youth, especially Black males, reject school because the type of information obtained there to them is lame since it fails to highlight the achievements of the heroes of the lower socio-economic students. Consequently, the students that embrace the teachings of primarily European heroes and achievers are called "nerds," "sell-outs" and "geeks" because they have mastered knowledge that is termed useless by the cool students. Of course, after years of such behavior, the cool students suffer from a self-inflicted academic form of retardation which forces them to act out in class since it is cooler to be seen as a *trouble-maker* than a *dummy*. Overheard outside an inner city high school at the start of the school day is the following dialogue:

> *"Yo, Jesse, let's not go to school today. I'm not beat"*
> *"Why, Sam? I mean, I'm not sick or anything."*
> *"Look man, those teachers are trying to make us like them."*
> *"Huh?"*
> *"You know . . . that old 'i' before 'e' except after 'c' crap. Who needs it?"*
> *"Okay, I'm down, but where we gonna go?"*
> *"Let's go to the mall."*
> *"I don't know. My mom has friends who work there. They'll tell."*
> *"Let's go to the movies."*
> *"With what? I'm broke, man. Plus I've seen bootleg tapes of everything."*
> *"Uh, well, let's walk around."*
> *"What? And get caught by Truancy?"*
> *"Damn, Jesse. What are you, a nerd, geek, brainiac, or poindexter?"*
> *"Huh?"*
> *"You must love school. C'mon then, we're gonna be late."*

Education is the source of many Black males' problems, since in *coolposing*, toughness, resistance to authority, teachers and education, are leading indicators of masculinity and the acceptance of authority brands one as a "sell out". Some Black males identifying with the dominant societal norms and standard academic values often suffer social rejection from male peers. These "Street corner" rituals teach Black males perception, feelings, dignity, pride, consideration, self-attachment, and self-expression, and they frequently adhere to the code of the street as a ritual or rite of passage into the "in-crowd". Rejection from the inner circle for reasons of high academic achievement, which flies in the face of the street code, would earn the young male the label of "sissy", "homo", "geek", "nerd", or worse.

Many male gender performances involve the continuous refusal of feminine qualities or behaviors, such as gaining recognition as a high academic achiever by making the Honor Roll. Some males consider performing well in school as characteristic of femininity or homosexuality and feel pressured to negatively alter their schoolwork, by leaving blank, answers they know, and by refusing to volunteer to read in public, when they have previously demonstrated that they possess good oral communication skills that have pleased both teachers and administrators. Peers frequently call other males feminine names, such as "punk", "corny", "fag", or "oreo" if seeing them doing well academically, which establishes an agreed upon "code of the school" that they adhere to almost religiously in seeking the acceptance of their peers. *Coolposing* and its related compulsive masculinity traits are highly regarded as reasons for the rejection of academics by some Black males, particularly the young.

By what sends the white kids, I ain't sent:
I know I can't be president.

What don't bug them white kids sure bugs me:
We know everybody ain't free.

Lies written down for white folks ain't for us a-tall:
Liberty And Justice-Huh!-For All?

—Langston Hughes

Few Black males who are fearful of rejection by their peers, can successfully manage both popularity and academic success. Students devalue education through a method of academic disidentification, where particularly Black males fail and feel all right, because school achievement is not the basis of their self-esteem. Despite the later rejection of education, Black students-males in particular-outperform everyone else up to age 7, with some sustaining the advantage until age 11.

By age 14, Black males are the worst school under-performers. Child psychologists find no known specific ethnic factors accounting for this unusual decline in academic achievement. In view of this puzzlement of the best social scientists, the academic decline is undoubtedly intentional and expressed as academic work being unfavorable to popular taken-for-granted ideas of masculinity, such as coolness. This unorthodox method of failing to remain cool is an example of the *paradoxical intention*, or the need to purposely confuse others, is an intriguing, yet destructive characteristic of coolness.

A Black male educational consultant with over 35 years experience shares his personal experience, which prevented him from being a victim of academic disidentification:

> *My education helped develop my leadership style, but the most important element was having a mother and a father at home, pushing me to go to college and be successful. My parents were instrumental in helping shape my mental strength, self-esteem and self-efficacy by talking to me as an equal; not as a subordinate. My environment played a role in my development; however my socialization aided in my ability to code-switch and adjust to various needs of the situation. I learned to dress appropriately and control the impression of others. My leadership style evolved from my college training, watching my mentors, and emulating some of the gang leaders of my youth, who were some of the smartest people I knew then. Gang leaders delegated responsibility to others, such as the "warlord," "runner of the old heads," "juniors," "midgets," "half-pints," etc.*

A cause or perpetuation of the resistance to school by young Black males in particular is the fact that they are more often diagnosed with attention deficit disorders, have higher dropout rates, have a higher representation in special education, repeat a grade more often, and are more often placed in alternative schools. The frustration from these problems, results in their acting out in class more often than girls do. Despite emerging research that finds boys can function in an actively loud environment much better than girls, have better discipline and fewer disruptions in single-sex situations, and participate more when away from girls, all-male schools are rarely considered.

The research on single-sex schools in America is limited; significantly, more is available for females than males. An Australian study of 270,000 students over a six-year period found that males in single-sex schools ranked 15 to 20 percentile points higher than their peers in coed schools.

Even though groups claiming the schools would violate state and federal law reject attempts at all-male schools, the possibility looms large that the rejections are disguised methods to continue the massive failure and ultimate destruction of young Black males.

Cool Math

Three men together on a convention checked into an inexpensive motel for a daylong seminar. The bellboy carried their luggage to their room and announced, "The cost of the room is $30 per day, and you can pay me now." The three men each gave the bellboy $10 and he gave them a receipt. Shortly afterward, the bellboy returned and announced, "The owner informed me that since you will be gone to the seminar most of the day, and will not get the full use of your room, he will only charge you $25 for the room. He gave me $5 back to return to you." The men were delighted, so each agreed to take back $1 and give the remaining $2 to the bellboy as his tip. Later, one of the men said to the others, "We initially paid $30 for the room. Then the bellboy returned $1 each to us, which means we paid $27 total, or $9 each. We gave the bellboy a $2 tip, which added to the $27, brings the total to $29. What happened to the other dollar?"

—Traditional

When educators fail to provide *concrete examples of abstract concepts* for Black males, they literally accelerate his failure. Ideas of a national conspiracy against poor and Black males receiving the quality education guaranteed them by the Constitution exists in the central characteristics of teaching the oppressed. Poor Black males are over-represented in classrooms that boast constant teacher direction and student compliance. Those who fear minorities and the poor most often use this teaching style, have low expectations for minorities and the poor, and due to their lack of experience, do not know the full range of instructional options available.

These meager standards lacking innovation guarantee that the students on the receiving end will not be very motivated, therefore they seek other means to show their intelligence.

Educational practices accepted for Black males and other minorities are intellectually sterile and provide dangerous half-truths, which deepens the divisions of a segregated school system. These segregated arrangements ensure that the more experienced instructors teach the privileged and the least experienced teach the minorities. School, therefore is not valued as the overriding determinant of rank within many inner city communities, yet youth respected intelligence in some form. While school tends to limit the curriculum focus to logical and computational skills, such as math and science, other less appreciated intelligences such as interpersonal, intrapersonal, kinetic, musical, spatial, ecological and humanitarian competences exist. Many youths place such an extremely high value on kinetic or athletic accomplishment that they frequently turn their backs on the classroom to pursue fame and fortune in the field of athletics, despite the miniscule odds of being successful.

A KNOCK ON THE BLACK JOCK

"Did you see the big game?"

"No, I missed it. How was it?"

"Oh, God, you should have seen Johnny."

"How many did he get?"

"He scored 100 points with time still on the clock."

"What? That's amazing!"

"Yeah, the sports announcers were tripping over each other."

"For real?"

"Yeah, Channels 3, 6, 10, 17, 29 and the Sports Channel were all there."

"Did they interview him?"

"Now, you know that boy can't speak well."

"Aren't his teachers working with him?"

"How? He rarely comes to class; he is always traveling to tournaments."

"He better get some speech help before he makes it to college."

"You mean to the pros don't you?"

"Oh, you're right; he will bypass college like all the others, then regret it."

"Right, just after he gets cut from the roster because he can't read the plays."

Inner city school districts such as Philadelphia, New York, Chicago, Detroit, Baltimore, Camden, and Washington D.C. consistently lead the nation in failure, with standardized scores at or near the bottom. What is less clear is how these same cities annually produce the finest crop of athletes in the nation. There is a growing trend of high school basketball players-such as Kobe Bryant, Darryl Dawkins, Moses Malone, Kevin Garnett and others-so accomplished that they regularly bypass college to become top draft choices of NBA teams. The intelligence required for the classroom is sacrificed to focus on the physical conditioning, muscle coordination drills, and hours of jump shooting necessary to succeed in the NBA.

There is a huge contradiction in *coolposing*; sports, the thing thought to provide a jumpstart to manhood, actually prolongs childhood. In sports, grown men become juveniles with nicknames such as "Bubba," "Night Train," "Cool Papa," "The Refrigerator," "White Shoes," "Hollywood," "Magic" "Sugar", "His Airness", "A-I" and "Superman" among others. There is disagreement in respecting nicknamed players of games for any purpose other than their exploits within the lines of the playing field, which is strictly for entertainment. Outside of these lines is where the real-world problem solving occurs, which is when society tend to call on certified and credentialed professionals such as clergy, doctors, lawyers, bankers, accountants, teachers, and plumbers; not athletes. After the final, career-ending whistle, the public sees a general uselessness for the athlete, especially those who have celebrated their 35th birthdays and beyond.

Past generations cheered the heroics of heavyweight champion Joe Louis giving Max Schmeling and Germany a first round headache that lasted for over 75 years, as a result of his famous knockout. After his career ended, and America's truth-twisting needs were fulfilled, which ended his usefulness, Louis was broke and reduced to work as a greeter at Las Vegas casinos. The following generations cheered baseball great, Willie Mays all the way to his final days when he played one season too many and began experiencing the mishaps of aging, such as stumbling around the base paths, misplaying routine flies, and too frequently striking out.

Today's generation watches athletic superstars too numerous to recall become prisoners and addicts, constantly making the headlines for stupid behavior often incapable of performing simple tasks, such as making flight arrangements, securing a room in the most conveniently located hotel, making out an agenda for their day, and paying taxes. These tasks were previously done for them by their coaches and others since their early teens. Much of the early idolizing and comps of star athletes disables them in later years.

Creative expression was a leading signifier of *coolposing*, yet; on the contrary, over-identification with athletes and physical performance limited the growth and development of many young and older Black males. Academic achievement was discouraged in favor of physical performance and this tendency too often led to the "dumb jock" syndrome of all brawn and no brains. Many professional athletes fail to secure a college degree and usually self-destruct when their playing days are over.

Cool behaviors of Black males in America have reached a level that deserves national concern; at the heart of the matter is the idea that the school failure rate, among other things, has been identified as an obstacle for the past ten years. Government funding has been applied to stop the "bleeding" in this crucial area needed for achievement. After various studies, there is an indication that the same achievement gap exists in the 2000s that existed in the 1990s, with no noticeable change. The evidence is growing that suggests this gap remains because it is intentional on the part of many of the Black males affected; in other words, because of the gratification they are receiving from their involvement in the *coolposing* culture of drugs, fine dressing, driving fast cars, dating, and different community drama, they refuse to release themselves from the hold of the addictive lifestyle of coolness.

Furthering the problem of coolposing behavior in the classroom is the tendency of young Black males to imitate successful comedians such as Chris Rock, Eddie Murphy, Martin Lawrence, Steve Harvey, Cedric "The Entertainer", and Katt Williams. These comedians rely on "ghetto" humor, which generally involves a put-down of some element of the Black community, such as single mothers, incarcerated fathers, addicted siblings, impoverished relatives, unemployed neighbors, down on their luck friends, the church, school failure, police abuse, teen pregnancy, AIDS, and other issues that affect many lives. Young, impressionable school children repeat the comedy routines in classrooms and use the off-task behavior to both get laughs and conveniently cover-up their academic weaknesses of poor reading and writing skills or failed math scores.

The comedians are making a legitimate living and are doing nothing wrong, however parents, guardians, relatives and others in supervisory positions need to be more involved in preventing school children from accessing these controversial comedy performances. Laughter is a wonderful release of emotion outside of the classroom-inside of the classroom is not the place for stand-up comedy. One of the coolest feelings many youngsters seek is to be the center of attention and the quickest way to get laughter is through jokes. Class clowning is destructive to the coolposing Black male who is too young and unaware that the exact same things that make him laugh in his carefree teens, will make him cry in his un- and underemployed twenties, due to poor education.

3

WHY BLACK MALES KEEP INVENTING NEW WAYS TO MOVE

No man is an island entire of itself. Every man is a piece of the continent, a part of the main . . . Any man's death diminishes me because I am involved in mankind. And therefore, never send to know for whom the bell tolls. It tolls for thee.

—John Donne

Some highly sought-after cool traditions are dysfunctional for Black males. Many Black males often behave in unacceptable ways to be *cool* or *hip*, such as seeking momentary pleasure by spending their limited resources on highly stylish yet frequently poorly made clothing, electronic gadgets and other faddish items. The practice of noticeable spending is a standard fixture in the *coolposing* culture yet it creates debt and poverty, which is the direct opposite of coolness. Despite their frequent low wages and unstable employment, many Black males customarily drive high-end cars that provide a successful image while causing financial strain that leads to stressful maneuvering to avoid repossessions. The poor decision-making brings about the idea of many groups that except for sex and physical strength Black males are powerless institutionally in America.

The lack of good traditional jobs is why some Black males seek businesses. They accept the basic masculine goals, norms, and standards of our society but unlike White males, Black males lack the means to achieve these goals. Attempts at legitimate jobs are for many Black males, met with insult, or lack of promotion. The American employment game for Black males, according to the standard rules does not lead to upward mobility, flexibility and stability.

Black males react to not getting the best jobs by developing coping strategies, such as coolness, for pride, dignity and a sense of worth in the midst of adversity. Trends in *wealth inequality* of Black males and others reflect changes in *income inequality*, with both increasing steadily over the last 40 years. Coolness gives some Black males control, strength, balance, stability, confidence, security and 21st century survival skills to manage the necessary front to tolerate-within the law-this sham of justice in the American workplace.

Leaders as prophets, priests, chiefs, and kings were symbols, representatives, and models in the Old and New Testaments, in Greek and Latin classics and throughout African antiquity. Myths and legends about great leaders were significant in the development of civilized societies, such as the Yoruba of western Nigeria, who believed coolness was the correct way to represent the self to others. Coolness is a part of character, and character is a substance of 5000 years of African custom. Black male leaders' task is to help define reality and recognize that their leadership evolves from the realness of self through their presence, rooted in African civilization and tradition.

New forms of leadership allow the means of expressing the self through signs of outstanding accomplishments that appear primarily among followers. Influence is the real meaning of leadership and culture is the primary source of the influence. Coolness can switch from a manly macho to an accomplished maestro, when skillfully managed to provide good leadership that is artfully orchestrated and not brutally enforced. One accepts his fate; unless someone or something convinces him to change scripts, which when influenced by African culture is the suggestion of coolness. The Black male of today has to "man-up" to the challenge of taking responsibility for his family, community, business and nation; he did it once and he can do it again.

Many cities such as Philadelphia, Baltimore, Phoenix and Camden, New Jersey experienced and are experiencing economic revivals by emphasizing quality of life industries that saw inner cities build stadiums, museums, downtown aquariums, and restore restaurants, entertainment and residential districts. Some Black male businessmen led organizations in economic development using inner strength, balance, stability, confidence, security and masculinity, developed from cool behavior which was obtained as a boyhood coping mechanism and refined in manhood. Tools for leadership can expand through cool. Innovation of coolness referred to the ability of *disciplined, self-restrained* leaders to create organizations to turn ideas into products and services, and successfully market them.

Cool has cut across social rank and therefore, given the ongoing systematic social, political and economic disrespect, Black Americans cover up their risky status by constructing *coolposing*. Creativity and imagination are the only limits in establishing the personal status based on posturing, fabrication and performance-oriented behaviors. Biased laws and access to quality jobs to prove their manhood denies some Black males a sense of manliness. As a result, once they are deprived of the means to own a stronghold, some Black males' minds have become mental forts, protected by watertight coolness.

Coolness provides many Black males with confidence, courage and the self-esteem necessary to compete in a world that has been historically hostile to them, and remains such. Adopting coolness provides emotional protection for many Black male businessmen that allow them to operate in marketplaces dominated by prejudice. Coolness is both structurally and functionally dynamic and involves roles, values, presentation of self, situation constructed and performance-oriented behaviors that relate to decision-making and leadership styles of Black males. Contemporary social conditions generate and support cool behaviors among Black males conducting business that show the dominant culture they are strong, proud and capable of survival despite their low status in society. Many Black males see cool behaviors as necessary for continued existence, and those seeking success as businessmen fashion a leadership pose that incorporates elements of business ownership and coolness, which sets into motion the strategies of *"Coolposing."*

BUSINESS OWNERSHIP AND COOLNESS SERVES BLACK MALES

"Watermelon, watermelon, red ripe watermelon, sweeter than before;

Watermelon, watermelon, red ripe watermelon, better than the store;

Watermelon, watermelon, red ripe watermelon, get yours right away;

Watermelon, watermelon, red ripe watermelon, come give me a play."

Sociologist William Edward Burghardt (W. E. B.) DuBois examined issues faced by Black male businessmen in his study of *The Philadelphia Negro*. DuBois examined decision-making and leadership styles of Black males, while exploring ways to improve living conditions in Philadelphia's mostly Black Seventh Ward. DuBois' research method was collecting data door-to-door and his questions to Black-owned businesses covered their operations, investments and leadership techniques.

The measurement instrument used by DuBois was a general survey with six categorical listings which he called *schedules*. DuBois' findings provided information of little known Black male leadership styles, decision-making and related strategies that opened a new world of knowledge and helped to positively change America's view of them. DuBois' findings suggested that being a man meant showing masculinity by taking care of his family. Ultimately, cool behavior appeared as exaggerated or ritualistic forms of masculinity controlled in part by the most prominent masculine role of the economic provider, known today as *paying the cost, to be the boss.*

Dubois found that Blacks never consciously trained for leadership in business; their constructed performance-oriented behaviors, personal scripts and physical posturing helped maintain the role of leader for some. He noted the lack of Black businessmen caused other groups to assume the inability of their leadership. DuBois showed that Black businessmen were not accustomed to doing business with other Blacks and he struggled to find reasons for the ongoing distrust of many Black merchants by Black consumers. The physical liberation for Blacks came in 1863 with the Emancipation Proclamation however the mental liberation came much later because many Black males have trouble trusting other Black males. In 2010, the lack of trust of one another is still a major issue among Black males, which is a major reason why Black on Black crime, especially murder, is rising.

Nguzo Saba
(Seven Principles)

1. *Umoja (Unity): To strive for and maintain unity in the family, community, nation, and race.*
2. *Kujichagulia (Self-determination): To define ourselves, name ourselves, create for ourselves, and speak for ourselves instead of being defined, named, created for, and spoken for by others.*
3. *Ujima (Collective Work and Responsibility): To build and maintain our community together, and to make our sisters' and brothers' problems our problems and solve them together.*
4. *Ujamma (Cooperative Economics): To build and maintain our own stores, shops and other businesses and to profit from them together.*
5. *Nia (Purpose): To make our collective vocation the building and developing of our community in order to restore our people to their traditional greatness.*
6. *Kuumba (Creativity): To do always as much as we can, in whatever way we can, in order to leave our community more beautiful and beneficial than we inherited it.*

7. *Imani (Faith): To believe with all our heart in our people, our parents, our teachers, our leaders, and in the righteousness and victory of our struggle.*

Because many Black consumers did not patronize Black merchants, economic emancipation, through effective leadership, was far off. Dr. Ron Karenga, the creator of the multi-ethnic holiday celebration of Kwanzaa, which is an alternative for those choosing not to celebrate Christmas, argues that Black masculinity training should emphasize the principles of the Afrocentric value system of *Nguzo Saba*, which encompasses seven core values. Karenga believes practicing unity, self-determination, collective work and responsibility, cooperative economics, purpose, creativity and faith reduce social problems and disunity among Blacks. Blacks did not commonly practice these values, which guide decision-making and leadership style, when DuBois conducted his study.

DuBois carried out the first known exploration and identification of decision-making and leadership styles of business Black males and duplicated his findings in *Report of a Social Study*. He refined the practice of door-to-door canvassing, sent questionnaires to 1,906 Black businessmen in 30 states, and presented a paper to the Fourth Conference for Study of Negro Problems, at Atlanta University, in 1899. DuBois' paper was accepted and promoted six resolutions.

1. *Negroes need to increase business endeavors.*
2. *The best-trained and educated Negroes need to enter business.*
3. *Negroes must give the best customer service in order to expect patronage from other members of the race.*
4. *Negroes need to learn to patronize Negro owned businesses, even if there are some slight disadvantages. (Race loyalty is a prerequisite for Black-owned businesses to thrive).*
5. *The Negro elite should set the example by supporting Negro businesses.*

6. *Emphasize the necessity of Negro businesses with youth and encourage business as a career choice; teach money management skills to youth; and organize Negro Business Men's Leagues in every city*

—W.E.B. DuBois

The accepted resolutions were the beginning of four findings of the Armstrong Association's study, which showed that Black business owners mostly were inexperienced, lacked training, lacked ability, and poor money management skills, which created difficulty in their securing loans. Following DuBois' study Armstrong gathered data on Black businessmen and found that Blacks in transition to Philadelphia from the South saw fewer job opportunities.

The Armstrong study built upon and extended aspects of DuBois' study of experience by seeking evidence of the tradition of Black business. Armstrong informed the existing studies of Black males by discovering the way participants think of what Majors has coined as *cool pose* in their everyday lives. Of special interest was the revelation that 21% of Black American business owners indicated they had relatives and ancestors who were businesspersons. The evidence of a strong African connection to business ownership helped reveal many techniques used by Black ancestors to make leadership decisions in past centuries (These techniques will be explored in a later chapter).

Most businesses were domestic service and barbershops, which grew out of social conditions brought on by oppression, destitution and desperation, rather than the purposeful search for knowledge. Black males often conducted business for very short periods and failed. The quick failure was largely due to being business newcomers with little or no experience with Philadelphia's conditions. Despite barriers encountered in establishing businesses, Blacks were optimistic about the futures of both their community and businesses.

The value of the early research of Black male businesses is its exposure of deficiencies such as inexperience, lack of training, lack of ability, and difficulty in securing capital. The lack of "Negro business men" to apprentice inexperienced and untrained newcomers remained the major cause of only a small number of Black men in business. This suggests that Black male businessmen seek information for development of business succession programs so businesses can pass down from one generation to the next, and stop ending up in sheriff's sales.

Successful businesses were those of businessmen either born in Philadelphia or had been in the city for some time. The economic success of Black businessmen is most often coordinated by the number of years the business has been in operation. Of significance is that both economic culture and social capital affect the outcomes of Black business owners. Therefore, the individuals that best understand how money works and maintain a network that will support them will flourish; all others will perish. The following information is significant since it helps dispel the myth that Black males have no business experience or legacy of business in either America or Africa: Noteworthy issues of a cigar storeowner include a Black male businessman successfully managing his shop despite the loss of his arm.

(a) A businessman demonstrated self-motivation by thriving with no business experience, (b) purchasing a house in which he did business, (c) maintained patrons of both races and, (d) saved on discounts by paying for supplies with cash. Armstrong focused on accounting, management, leadership, organization, planning, and customer service skills. These were less known aspects of Black male businessmen in 1919.

—The Armstrong Association

A second case is a building contractor who showed evidence of the doubted Black business heritage, which included sound practices of Black male business leadership.

Armstrong documented perseverance-the businessman in the sample case never gave up after finding it hard to get work at his trade. His corporate management skills showed as a businessman and employer of 50 workers and handler of over $50,000. The building contractor exhibited cool behavior as a coping style to manage the inescapable psychological phenomenon of stress.

—The Armstrong Association

The financial skills in the building contractor's case were "exceptionally fine credit" and monthly balanced accounts. The leadership skill of a participant who maintained a prosperous business and continued to receive praise of his patrons helps debunk the myth that Black males are not personable businessmen. Longevity in his contracting business for ten years supported the business history of Blacks that revealed success and mastery of all phases of business at every level.

The third case is a tailor who is the first college graduate documented. Since there is no significant difference between educational backgrounds with regard to stress, cool behaviors, as coping mechanisms, was best suited for his use.

The tailor served his apprenticeship at a university, under the guidance of trained and credentialed instructors. What is noted is he had a business, which he left to improve himself by coming to Philadelphia. The tailor represented the much-doubted businessmanial heritage of Blacks which involved risk-taking to advance one's self. This example is central as it showed a Black male businessman's decision-making and leadership style move him towards self-actualization.

—The Armstrong Association

A grocer in the fourth case demonstrates little known characteristics of Black male businessmen: industriousness. The grocer gave evidence that research on family business influence deserves further study. Numerous researchers have found that the probability for the son of a self-employed man being self-employed and the probability for the son of a man who was not self-employed to be self-employed was much lower for Blacks than for Whites. The Black grocer defied the findings of these researchers.

The cigar storeowner, contractor, tailor and grocer showed they used factors that overcame societal barriers. Whether the barriers were bias, lack of skills and training, capital or intangibles, the one-armed cigar storeowner with no experience was successful by close personal application.

Current Black male businessmen practices are seen in the over 90 years-old study, which identified behaviors central to decision-making and leadership styles. The past cases were those who traveled to Philadelphia from the South and the western part of Pennsylvania, ran businesses as trades rather than professions, and their managed cash did not approach six figures. The following case shows how coolposing leadership of Black Males was present in 1917 in managing a bank that had assets over six figures.

The bank showed a gross business of $178,304.01 as of August 21, 1918. The real estate owned by the two proprietors amounts to $102,600.00, with a surplus and undivided profits of $20,162.48. This represents a remarkable growth when compared with the statement as of January 21, 1917, at which time the total resources were $10,728.62. This bank employs five young Colored women and two young men as tellers, clerks, bookkeepers, etc. In addition, the proprietors render service, one of the partners being cashier. In addition to the banking business, they also do a large real estate brokerage business. The bank is centrally located and is splendidly equipped. Before engaging in banking, here one of the partners conducted banks successfully in two cities in Virginia. The other partner was for some time in insurance and real estate brokerage business.

This bank has a large number of White depositors. The upper floors of the bank building are apartments and occupied by a select class of White tenants.

—The Armstrong Association

The two partners achieve more success by not falling prey to the limited purchasing power of residents in a very narrow parameter that constrains the potential of their business enterprises to expand. Three hundred thousand dollars in business gross, surplus and profits managed by two Black male businessmen in 1917 is less known among today's business owners. These compiled facts and information about Black inventors and businessmen help to conclude that no one can now contend that Blacks lack a business tradition. The original contribution of this information about Black male business behaviors connects strongly to the thinking within coolposing, which influences leadership, decision-making and leadership styles. The following chapter shows the foundation for the leadership strategies necessary to move the Black male businessman forward in business by providing a style that is balanced with the African culture, inherent in his life, both at work and home.

4

WHERE BLACK MALES' RHYTHM COMES FROM

It seems to me that there are two kinds of trickery: the "fronts"
people assume before one another's eyes, and the "front" a
writer puts on the face of reality.

—Francoise Sagan

One of the more remarkable examples of a unique leadership pose was recognized at the beginning of the twentieth century by Colonel Allen Allensworth. He was the founder of Allensworth; the only Black town ever built in California. Allensworth was born in Louisville, Kentucky on April 7, 1842. As soon as he was twenty-one years old, he fled slavery and joined the United States Army. He served in the Army until 1906 and when he retired, he took his family to settle in Los Angeles. Allensworth made his home in an area around a depot connecting Los Angeles to San Francisco on the Santa Fe rail line, which became California's first Black town.

The depot, called Solito, was renamed Allensworth. The town became a school district in 1912, incorporating thirty-three square miles. In 1914, the town became a judicial district and two residents, Oscar Overr and William H. Dotson, became the first Black men in California history to hold elected offices as justice of the peace and constable, respectively. Colonel Allensworth died in Los Angeles in 1914 when a motorcyclist struck him as he stepped off a streetcar. The town of Allensworth survived until 1966 when officials discovered suspiciously high levels of arsenic in the town's well water; it became a state historical site on May 14, 1976.

The value of Allensworth, who was born into slavery, is that he succeeded as well as few free men had. He conquered racial, economic and political barriers to flourish as a business and civic leader. Allensworth negotiated with a U.S. President, elected officials and fellow businessmen with decision-making skills and a leadership style influenced by his need for stability and flexibility in the midst of crises. Through reflection and analysis, significant meaning can be made of Allenworth's leadership experience that can support the need of a coolposing managing style for achieving positive objectives. He used coolness as a life sustaining invisible force in achieving the final state of less restricted men and overcame diverse conditions in different ways. His story showed the decision-making and leadership style influenced by coolness, present in many Black male businessmen.

My research recommends contact from employers for young Black workers who want business opportunities and that public schools introduce courses in place of apprenticeships frequently denied young Blacks. When denied, many Black males resort to coolposing behavior to demonstrate visibility and to avoid "zero" images. Black males, who fail to provide for their families, often will incorporate coolposing behavior to provide pride and masculinity to mask their denial of the pain and frustration of feeling inadequate.

Documenting little known Black male behaviors builds the heritage of business ownership that is necessary to pass down to youth and those who are newly entering business. Understanding culture through observation and documentation can help capture Black males' unique values and social processes of years ago. The knowledge of the past helps to fill some of the gap in the leadership literature that currently exists about decisions of business minded Black males.

MAJORS BEHAVIORAL STUDY OF BLACK MALES

"I don't care about that job. I can make more money hustling at night. Those people at that office can kiss my ass!" The man saying those words is most likely lying-he wanted the job badly, cannot make illegal money for long without going to jail, and attempts to hide his disappointment through *trash talking*. The complexity of coolposing deepens when it is used to shield against exploitation.

Playing it cool is a real and necessary strategy. The individual, in order to maintain internal balance and to protect himself from being overwhelmed by it, must initiate coolness in order to keep functioning-all quite automatic and unconscious. In addition to maintaining an internal balance, the individual must continue to maintain a front and some kind of adjustment to the problem that is getting him down so that he can preserve some public success.

Dr. Richard Majors provided the primary work on coolness and its relation to Black male behavior through his Ph.D. dissertation titled *Cool pose: A New Approach toward a Systematic Understanding and Study of Black Male Behavior*. Majors published a book titled, *Cool Pose: The Dilemmas of Black Manhood in America*. The dissertation and book are complements that provide ideas of the ongoing dilemmas of Black males.

Majors viewed coolposing as a way to help Black males adapt to environmental conditions, neutralize or safely contain stress and reduce anxiety. He explained cool posing as attempts to develop ways that maintain and enhance life and serve as defense mechanisms to deal with difficult situations. Defense mechanisms distort, disguise and deny motives, perceptions and other psychological contents, which historically, Black men have used to shield them from many forms of failure.

Coolposing is a part of character, and character is the representation of one's self in everyday life. The occurrence of cool has played an important role in the historical, social and cultural development of Black people, especially some Black males. Some Black male businessmen use cool behaviors to fight against stress caused by meaningful life supporting social, economic, political, and business issues.

Psychology and social science practically ignored *cool* as a legitimate topic of research. Scholars did not previously consider the subject of cool to be important enough to merit significant subject indexing. As a result, the lack of research on cool determined Majors' choice to study the subject and pioneer scholarly and systematic research on Black males and cool.

I fought with fists and lost them all
Some to the great and some to the small

I fought with guns and lost those too
My shots rang wide, my foe's rang true

I fought with words spoke with my tongue
I'm speechless now, with a wounded lung

I fight with thoughts and write them down
Finally, I wear the victor's crown!

—Dr. George Cross, DM

Majors' study is important to this book. Some Black male business leaders can use aspects of coolposing to guard against various forms of stress, oppression, conflict and marginalizing from the dominant business culture. Black men's anger is often misunderstood, and through the exploration and identification of experience, both stylistic and substantive differences can arise when compared with previous studies about men.

The effects of coolposing on leadership decisions of Black males inform others and contribute to understanding the individual differences in leadership competencies. Perceptions, thoughts and emotions that are revealed through actual experience offer original knowledge of less known aspects of Black male leaders. One can better understand Black male businessmen functioning in the 21st century once he or she knows the business origin of the Black male which actually goes all the way back to America's birth.

ORIGINS OF BLACK BUSINESS LEADERSHIP

"I have these fox skins, bear furs, and spices to trade."
"I'm interested. I could use my skills with wood to build cabinets for you in exchange."
"Can you build an addition to my barn?"
"Yes. You can pay me with some of the food that you grew."
"Well, maybe you can build me a little store."
"Okay, and instead of paying me, I'll be your partner."
"Um, I'll think about it."
"By the way, what is your name?"
"Pierre DuSable"
"And where do you live?"
"On that river bank that I call *Chicago*."
Black people had business spirit and business involvement before the Trans-Atlantic Slave Trade; their business ownership developed in North America during the decade after the American Revolution, in 1776. The first documented protest against slavery was in Philadelphia in 1688, followed by the organization of the Pennsylvania Abolition Society. During this time free Africans were building, trading and selling with the specific purpose of uplifting Blacks from circumstances, forced on them.
Free sailors of color turned to the sea to make a living in coastal trading. Black New Englanders, in 1788, were independently earning livelihoods, holding families together, acquiring property and gaining respect. One hundred and fifty years earlier, the first known Black businessman, Anthony Johnson came to America in 1621 from England. Johnson imported and paid for five servants, which determined he be granted 250 acres of land

under the *headright system*. The headright system permitted planters to claim fifty acres of land for each person they brought to the colony of Jamestown, Virginia.

Johnson and his relatives established one of America's first Black communities along the Pungoteague River. It is significant to mention here that Anthony Johnson was real, not make believe, and his existence can be verified through documentations that are available for all who are interested. The Pungoteague River where he lived and worked is mentioned in a 1700s document about a West Indian planter named "Willie Lynch" that describes the best method to colonize and control African slaves. The letter has been well circulated throughout America and is simply called "The Willie Lynch Letter". The letter was referenced by religious leader Louis Farrakhan in October 1995 on the Washington Mall during the famous "Million Man March". Fortunately, scholars have thoroughly researched the letter and have determined, beyond a doubt, that it is a fake.

The "Willie Lynch" letter tells of strategies such as separating the light complexioned from the dark, the young from the old and the weak from the strong to create division among Africans. It describes divisive ways to control and frighten Black people. Through solid research the letter was proven a fraud because it mentioned words that had not yet been created at that time, and there were numerous errors in the mention of directions in which the ship sailed, such as "sailing south on the Pungoteague River" when in fact the ship was supposedly coming up from the south. In addition, if a letter is that prominent that it was preserved since the 1700s, something should have been mentioned in one of the local papers in Virginia, or the surrounding area. This did not happen-there has been no verifiable evidence that "Willie Lynch" ever existed. There is no recorded mention in any paper, pamphlet, journal, diary, log, handbill, flyer, or other letters.

The attempt of the letter was to caution Black people, males especially, that they had better be careful of colonization and control of a dominant group. The phony letter attributed to Willie Lynch was found to be circulated over the Internet by some college students in 1993. The race of the students is unknown. Hopefully, there will be no more circulation of the "Willie Lynch" urban tale to further confuse many about myth and reality.

The first generation of Blacks had about the same industrial or economic opportunities as free White servants. Many Black businessmen were able to serve soldiers in time of battle and help turn the tide of the Revolutionary War. A major attraction for Blacks during the Revolutionary War was the promise by the British that they would be granted their freedom regardless of the war's outcome.

Blacks have been a part of the labor force that built the United States since the 1700s. Lesser known is the recognition of Black male leadership in the economic development of America. Wall Street is the most famous financial symbol of America, and the United States Capitol Building and the White House are two of the most prominent symbols of the United States government. American Black males played major roles in building all three structures.

Blacks, laboring as slaves, worked on the first stage of the United States Capitol's construction from 1793 to 1802. The United States Government paid their owners five dollars per month per slave. Blacks also did much of the work in constructing Pierre Charles L'Enfant's design of the District of Columbia.

President George Washington dismissed L'Enfant because of a serious dispute concerning ideas about the design. L'Enfant, angry and resentful, took all of his designs with him. Benjamin Banneker, a Black man, was a surveyor laying boundaries of the District of Columbia who recalled most of the designs from memory, and completed the final work. Blacks cleared the forest between sites of the Capitol building and the White House, which required much independent and collaborative work. Black men led many work teams by experience in decision-making and knowledge of the appropriate leadership style to complete the important tasks.

BLACK MALE LEADERSHIP DURING THE AMERICAN REVOLUTION

"Halt, who goes there?"

"It's only me, the stable boy."

"Oh, it's the nigger. He's safe, poor thing. Go on across."

"(Under his breath) Ah, it worked like a charm. As soon as I get near the tent where the enemy troops are, I will set off the dynamite that is loaded in this wagon and the American chances to win this war will be greatly improved (Hee hee)."

Black male businessmen were responsible for many less known acts of bravery. Valley Forge, Pennsylvania, was the site of General George Washington's encampment and grounds of many historic recorded deeds. Cyrus Bustill, a Black baker from Philadelphia, after who Bustleton Avenue is named, brought bread to Valley Forge for starving armies and Rev. Richard Allen, a business leader, church founder and one of the most respected Black men of his day, brought salt and supplies from Rehoboth, Delaware to Washington's troops at Valley Forge. Without the valuable provisions under dangerous conditions provided by Black males such as these, it is highly likely that Washington's troops would not have been victorious.

Enslaved Blacks such as Pompey, James Armistead, and Salem Poor (whose name was actually Saleem, and was a Muslim) began invaluable service as spies and independent contractors. It is necessary to mention that Salem, or rightfully Saleem, relied heavily on his Muslim religion and upbringing to proudly perform in the service of Allah and his country simultaneously. Muslim Blacks, who figured prominently in the early defense of this country have been essentially written out of American history, however it is well documented that at least 60 percent of the over 10 million kidnapped Africans were Muslims. Many sheds and shacks of abandoned slave quarters in various southern states revealed unmistakable Arabic etchings on the walls. There were numerous Korans discovered through the periodic searches of slave quarters by overseers as well as Islamic symbols and references on grave stones.

The Muslim, Poor got credit for taking down a British officer in the Battle of Bunker Hill, Pompey contributed to the victory of the Continental forces under General "Mad Anthony" Wayne, and Armistead was a celebrated master spy who played a significant role in forcing the surrender of the British General Cornwallis.

Prince Whipple, a Black bodyguard to General Whipple of New Hampshire, served as an oarsman with General George Washington. Whipple was in a small rowboat that crossed the Delaware River on Christmas Day in 1776. Whipple, is in the front of the boat in the historic paintings and drawings of Washington crossing the Delaware that symbolize adventure, courage, risk taking and business spirit of America. Blacks demonstrated business sense and patriotic spirit by being involved with the building of America, including Wall Street.

When American thieves loaded the first slave ships
   Black Music also made that trip
   And though the voyage across was inhumane
   Black Music helped relieve the pain

   When the economy dropped from the stock market dive
   Black Music kept a whole race alive
   So, when nuclear war causes global death . . .
   Black Music will be all that's left.

         —Dr. George Cross, DM

  Blacks had no way to enter business on the same level of Whites because Blacks had no *known* business legacy. Despite having to overcome staggering odds, Black ancestors, traded on the auction blocks located on Wall Street during the 1700's, used their skills as artisans and craftsmen and helped build Wall Street. For Black people, their first participation with stocks and bonds came from the client side, which is that of slaves kept in the *stock*yard and shackled with *bonds*.

  Black ownership in equities and emerging Black professionals trying to master the rules of investing traces back to the 1800s. The New York African Society for Mutual Relief owned $500 in bank stock in the mid-1800s. Also in the mid-1800s, Stephen Smith, a wealthy Black lumber merchant from Philadelphia, was the largest shareholder in a thrift named Columbia Bank.

  A Black man tried to buy a seat on the then young but flourishing New York Stock Exchange (NYSE) before the start of the Civil War. The NYSE refused the Black man's offer. Business spirit existed among Black males for centuries. Denials and limitations led Blacks to build businesses in their own communities.

  Restriction forced Black residents of many communities, such as Tulsa, Oklahoma, to realize the power of ownership. In the late 1800s and early 1900s, there were 1,500 Black-owned businesses in a 35-block span of Tulsa known as the Greenwood District. Among the residents of the Greenwood District were 10 millionaires and many families with substantial savings. The Greenwood District grew wealthy because of economic development and became the "Negro Wall Street". An unsubstantiated claim of sexual assault of a White woman resulted in the Tulsa Race Riot of 1921 that destroyed Negro Wall Street. Hundreds of lives and millions of dollars were lost with the destroyed symbol of Black self-reliance and success.

The business spirit that created the "Negro Wall Street" of Tulsa relied on specific traits and characteristics that include high motivation, organizational skills, innovation, management skills, high self-esteem, and determination. Less known is how Black proprietors were able to develop the necessary business skills. Missing is a thorough understanding of coolposing and its influence on business leadership skill development of Black males that is revealed in a later chapter.

Given their histories of underclass status, less education, inferior business skills and generations of poverty, how do Black male businessmen effectively lead businesses? How do Black businessmen find more than nominal success in conquering barriers to business opportunities? Research is lacking on business minded Black males' attitudes, values, beliefs and perceptions required for successfully overcoming the challenges of business leadership. The mastery of *coolposing* appears to be worthwhile in the face of evidence that the historical mimicry of past leadership strategies based on a European model have proven to be disastrous to Black males.

EARLY INVENTIONS WHICH LED TO BLACK MALE BUSINESSES

"Calvin, my back is hurting from moving this heavy sofa."

"You better stop complaining, Massa said we have five more to move."

"Five more!? I don't think I can make it. These things are heavy."

"Wait a minute. Look over there."

"Where?"

"There. See that broken baby carriage?"

"Yeah."

"Quick, let's take the wheels off of it."

"And do what?"

"And put them under this heavy sofa, fool."

"Oh, so it can coast easier?"

"Yeah. I just invented *coasters*".

Blacks found necessity and freedom to be the most important factors that inspired their contributions to inventions. Freedom meant that creative Black males could have their works patented. Blacks recorded more than three hundred patents in 1871-1900 and many of their patents developed during the "Great Enslavement" existed even when slavery ended.

The inventive spirit of Black males is even more remarkable when it is realized that much of the Black population could not then and cannot now read nor write. Many Black inventors had patents claimed by dishonest lawyers and so-called friends who took advantage of them. Many Blacks, instead of securing patents for themselves, sold their rights and patents to Whites.

One inventor, who eventually sold his patent, made history in the process. He is Garrett A. Morgan, born in 1887 and lived until 1963. He was an exceptionally bright inventor, creating several products of benefit to society. Morgan's gas inhalator proved to be effective against smoke when he rescued several men in Cleveland while wearing the inhalator. Hundreds of orders came in for the inhalator from fire companies throughout the United States. When southerners found out that the inventor was Black, they often cancelled their orders.

In the First World War, the gas inhalator became a gas mask, as Morgan sought to profit from its value. Unwilling to take a chance that prejudice against his race would stop his plans to market his most famous invention, Morgan sold his automatic traffic light invention to the General Electric Company for $40,000. Morgan's innovations are used every day and the source of his ideas, like his name, remains unknown to many. Morgan achieved the final state: accomplishment. He found success by crossing a different route under different conditions and in different ways, by resorting to tactics of coolness.

Morgan achieved the inventions of the gas mask and automatic traffic light through aspects of a soul-like factor, which governs processes in foresight of the goal. Like other Black men, Morgan used inexplicable vital phenomena, such as developing marketable inventiveness under oppressed conditions, to overcome societal barriers to leadership. The overcoming of barriers through unconventional methods is a central aspect of coolness, which allows the misdirection, inversion, fronting and masking needed to disguise one's true intention.

This section focused on strategies of decision-making and leadership styles of Black male businessmen; less known are methods of motivation that inspired many Black male inventors to pursue their creations and persevere.

This invention section concludes with the Blacksmith. Blacksmiths particularly were responsible for fashioning new inventions in order to make work on farms easier. Often one enslaved person would take an idea to a Blacksmith for creation to perform certain tasks. The majority of effective inventions were through creative efforts to lessen the drudgery of an enslaved person's work.

With little documented business or engineering training, Blacksmiths often maintained foresight of the goal and accomplished drudgery-reducing inventions in different ways. This is accomplishment through a soul-like factor maintained in behaviors seen in ritualized cool roles of some Black males in leadership positions. What remains unknown yet perhaps knowable is the role of cool on influencing Black male leadership. [See more inventions in the Index sction]

MYTH, MYTHICISM AND MYSTIQUE OF BLACK MALES AND COOLNESS

This section focuses on the connection of myth, mystique, mysticism and coolness, which combine to make many Black males seem very strange to society in general. The interpretation of the mysterious presence found within coolposing remains a fleeting idea of this book. Through the examination of records of culture-specific behavior necessary for established routine and rituals that seek social capability, it may be discovered why for some people, cool is not a way of life; it is life.

The attitude of cool, with its mystique, goes back to ancient civilizations that were the foundations of life. These civilizations, which are recorded as the beginnings of life over two million years ago, are from which Africans came west by way of the slave trade. Black musicians and jazz music retained much of this ancient mystique and kept the modern version of cool alive until Hollywood scriptwriters and crime writers of the 1930s and 1940s exposed it for money making purposes. Elvis Presley and rock and roll later injected a diluted version of *cool* into White culture.

Since African culture is not formed by materialism, the authentic cool remained in place as a bastardized version went commercial. Mystic cool, or what was left of it, found its way into the beat generation, rock, soul, funk, hip-hop and various newer forms of creative expression. Toni Morrison combined folklore, history, memory and mysticism into unforgettable meditation on race, in her novel, Sula, as she noted:

> I mean, I don't know what the fuss is about. I mean, everything in the world loves you. White men love you. They spend so much time worrying about your penis they forget their own . . . And White women? They chase you all to every corner of the earth, feel for you under every bed . . . Colored women worry themselves into bad health just trying to hang on to your cuffs. Even little children-White and Black, boys and girls-spend all their childhood eating their hearts out 'cause they think you don't love them. And if that ain't enough, you love yourselves. Nothing in the world loves a Black man more than another Black man . . . It looks to me like you the envy of the world.

The above passage describes an imagined image and promotes racial stereotypes that cannot save Black males from their modern image. Athletic achievement has done little to transform the original positive image of Black men. The current stereotypes represent entrance into business of Black males and is not an effective public image. Some Black males have adopted distinctive actions and attitudes described emphasizing respect, virility and physical strength to maintain pride while faced with economic castration and political trauma.

Public images of sensible Black men do not exist. Myth never really was and is the issue to overcome by Black men struggling to free themselves of negative outside images. Somehow, myth always is, even though it is a lie.

Black males have to spiritually and mystically survive those mean yesterdays, when they lost so much, including property, money, jobs, and family. The confidence to manage all kinds of situations that lead to survival is the mystic coolness. This mystical behavior identifies those experiences beyond human understanding and fills persons with spiritual insight, enlightenment, or extreme happiness.

Coolness is mythical in our imagination, and a part of our character, and it also makes it clear what the proper customs are. Coolness becomes intelligence and it leads to consumption or things that we buy, as advertisers create a constantly updated mix of styles and entertainments designed to affect the way we think about ourselves and society. Mystique exists in the exploration of cultural and the mental tradition in cool decision-making and leadership styles.

DuBois reasoned that some Blacks' double consciousness resulted from being gifted with second sight. Second sight, according to DuBois, is a sign of the peculiar ability to see beyond the ordinary. Many Black male businessmen and others, through second sight, reject traditional masculine ideas so there is now a masculinity crisis in which many feel bewildered and confused. They seek mystical or even magical methods that can only be found in being cool in order to return them to their rightful place as the leaders of their families.

Part of the mystique of some Black males guide them to offer advice that probably is from across thousands of years of time and miles of space. Some Black males are aware of the myth that remembers paradise and a time when communication between heaven and earth was possible. Being cool creates a link between the worlds of the past and future, heaven and hell, and even, life and death. This is the power of being not just cool; way past cool.

Many Black male businessmen use coolposing and its mystical energy to both oppose humiliation and at the same time push their way into the wallets of young consumers. Some Black males gain the balance between the two worlds of learning the trauma to greater life with access to great power at great risk. Attempting to cope through cool behaviors in business challenges Black male businessmen to not lose themselves in the three personality traits of cool which are narcissism (being stuck on one's self), hedonism (wanting only pleasure), and ironic detachment (not caring about people or things).

DuBois understood the mystique of Black males when in *The Souls of Black Folk* he showed they expressed *unvoiced longing toward a truer world*. Black males withdrew the forces that shaped their perceptions from history, and relocated them in their minds. By developing their unique perceptions of themselves, many Black males formed a permanent, private and individual concept of cool. A general definition of cool is *a permanent state of private rebellion*. Based on this definition, Black males are always against something that is not right, such as the law, schools, banks, hospitals, business, jails, religion, and politicians.

Through coping skills and survival styles, Black male businessmen overcome societal barriers to leadership. The negative stereotypes of Black males appear constantly in both movies and television. The following is a review by writer Bogle of the negative stereotypical images that are used in film and television that the Black male has battled:

The Tom:

The Tom is chased, harassed, hounded, flogged, enslaved, and insulted. They keep the faith, never turn against their White masters and remain hearty, submissive, stoic, generous, selfless and oh-so-very kind. They endear themselves to White audiences as heroes of sorts.

The Coon:

The coon developed into the most blatantly degrading of all Black stereotypes. The pure coon emerged as a no account nigger. Those unreliable, crazy, lazy, subhuman creatures good for nothing more than eating watermelons, stealing chickens, shooting craps or butchering the English language.

The Tragic Mulatto:

The tragic mulatto symbolized the fair skinned Black trying to pass for White. Usually the mulatto is likable (because of their [sic] White blood) and the audience believes that their life can have been productive and happy had they not been the victims of divided racial inheritance.

The Buck:

Bucks are always big, brutal oversexed Black men.

The above listed negative stereotypical images of Black men often found in media prompted them to use their own healing abilities for the purpose of mental and social conflict resolution:

In Afro America, one observes not only singular individuals but also . . . larger agencies of psychosocial cure. In its life and death struggle with the disorders generated by the oppression of racism like deteriorating self-esteem, internalized feelings of inferiority, and intergroup mistrust," the Black community has evolved forms of corporate shamanism (a high form of individualized mysticism).

The above passage identifies the force present in movements, and any healing practice formed through one-on-one relationships, families, places of worship, community organizations, boycotts, labor strikes, protests and victory celebrations. The power of the spiritual or mystical ability of the Black male, as a result of ancestral communication can be felt or witnessed in some other manner when understood in relation to issues and situations:

> That practices social and political visions display spiritual dynamics. At the heart of such a dynamic is an inter-linkage of social change and personal transformation. The spiritual factor emerges any time a vision begins to function as a device for inviting us to make ourselves over in the image of the imagery.

Mystical references of spiritual dynamics and factors provide devices that encourage Black males to make themselves over in the image of the new and improved imagery. In other words, when Black males say, "I am going through changes," they mean it as realistically as possible. Role-playing, which is essential to coolness, is a major concern when keeping up a front as a coping mechanism against workplace bias. Black men have nobly acted to coolly create mental and physical transformation by not only wearing the mask of their choosing, they also make known the essential being of the powers infused into them through the representation of the mask. Therefore, the role-play turns around; they play the role.

The spirit of the shaman (magic man), medicine man, or priest with magic powers who cast out evil spirits or brings good through dances, feasts, or chants, is present where groups of Black men gather. The territory of the shaman is a world of ideas, especially about the unknown. Some peoples believe shamans communicate directly with spirits. Paul Laurence Dunbar expressed spirit of the shaman-like Black writer with his poem, "The Poet":

> He sang of life, serenely sweet,
> With, now and then, a deeper note.

From some high peak, nigh, yet remote,
He voiced the world's absorbing beat.

He sang of love when earth was young
And love itself was in his lays.
But ah, the world, it turned to praise
A jingle in a broken tongue.

GRIOTS, POETS, AND WRITERS INSTRUMENTAL IN EARLY BLACK LITERARY TRADITION

The word *griot*, French term of unknown origin, became popular for expert in oral interpretive performance throughout West Africa. The term continues for poets and writers who contributed great warnings among topics. According to Benjamin:

> Scipio Moorehead, enslaved Black artist, poet, and friend of Ms. Wheatley's living in Boston, drew the frontispiece portrait of poet, Phyllis Wheatley depicting her with quill in hand. Although Blacks knew colonial American culture at least as early as 1619 in Jamestown, Virginia, this engraving with its published appearance in 1773 is the first appearance in our national culture of the image of a Black identified by name.

Benjamin identified little known history by a poet/writer in the role of historian, genealogist, spokesperson and teacher. The *New York Times* called Paul Laurence Dunbar "a true singer of the people-Black or White", and praised his success as the first known Black male businessman marketing poetry and writing. Dunbar was the first Black poet to achieve national recognition. He demonstrated empowerment and self-help as the only Black student in his class and became class president and class poet. Dunbar's first collection of poems was published with assistance of former classmate: Orville Wright, airplane pioneer.

Frederick Douglass wrote a letter to his former slave master, Thomas Auld that conveyed empowerment and self-help:

Sir-I have selected this day on which to address you, because it is the anniversary of my emancipation; knowing no better why, I am led to this as the best mode of celebrating that truly important event. Just ten years ago this beautiful September morning, yon bright sun beheld a slave-a poor, degraded chattel-trembling at the sound of your voice lamenting that I was a man, and wishing myself a brute. The hopes which I had treasured up for weeks of a safe and successful escape from your grasp, were powerfully confronted at this last hour by dark clouds of doubt and fear, making my person shake and my bosom heave with the heavy contest between hope and fear. I have no words to describe to you the deep agony of soul, which I experienced, on that never to be forgotten morning—(for I left by daylight.) I was making a leap in the dark. The probabilities, so far as I can by reason determine them, were stoutly against the undertaking. The preliminaries and precautions I had adopted previously, all worked badly. I was like one going to war without weapons-the chances of defeat to one of victory. One in whom I had confided, and one who had promised to assistance, appalled by fear at the trial hour, deserted me, thus leaving the responsibility of success or failure solely with myself. You, sir, can never know my feelings. As I look back to them, I can scarcely realize that I have passed through a scene so trying. Trying however as they were, and gloomy as was the prospect, thanks be to the Most High, who is ever the God of the oppressed, at the moment which was to determine my whole early career. His grace was sufficient; my mind was made up. I embraced the golden opportunity, took the morning tide at the flood, and a free man, young, active and strong, is the result.

Early Black seafaring autobiographers showed pride in African cultural and geographic origins. Blacks defined themselves in opposition to societies where they lived. Theirs was the opening salvo in a barrage of literature by Black authors dedicated to liberation. This early collective of Black writers sought reason greater than reality: the power of spirit.

LITERATURE GAPS

Masculinity is a social construction and ideals of manhood may differ for men of different social classes, races, ethnic groups, sexual orientations, life stages, and historical eras. A gap exists in understanding how cool relates to masculinity issues of Black business leaders that can affect decision-making and leadership styles.

Rather than racial discussion of Black failure, the need is to interpret Black male business ownership where it clearly flourishes. Shifting away from traditional industries to Black enterprise that maintains Black-controlled economies can begin to question patterns of ongoing Black business. *Hip-hop* music is just one very good instance of a wider process, which has enabled Black male businessmen decision-making and leadership styles to establish a culture producing goods taken for granted in the early twenty-first century. Role models such as businessmen Sean Combs and Jay-Z are positive images for young Black males to follow. They are the latest examples to carry on a strong history of Black business ownership.

Black male businessmen demonstrated leadership, despite barriers, before the Trans-Atlantic Slave Trade. Black males are part of the labor force that built the United States since the 1700s. Black men played major roles in building the most prominent symbols of United States government: Capitol Building, White House and District of Columbia. Lesser known is how Black businessmen developed the necessary leadership skills given their history of underclass status, less education, inferior business skills and generations of poverty.

For enslaved Blacks, reading and writing was more than a symbol of freedom; it was freedom. The exploration of griots, poets and writers provides much information about myth, mysticism and the mystique of Black culture. Leadership skills of Black males may be the end result of the influence of culture and cool.

The original contribution of this book is the documentation of little known Black male behaviors, which can influence decision-making and leadership styles. Black male businessmen found that more than a few business successes answered the questions of influence, and leadership.

The findings of the research for this book reveal that the appropriate attitudes by Black males helped them to understand the ongoing leadership challenges of their group.

Black males can bring out the best in their children by sharing the most precious things in the world-truth and love.
(Courier-Post)

Coolposing children are always watching their fathers and other
Black males, because they, along with many others believe
the black male is the envy of the world.
(Vincent Smith)

My oldest son, George Cross, IV who is a doctor, ABD, is living proof that children go forward and what they see they become.
(Kyle V. Cross)

John Coltrane, who played a spiritual form of Jazz, is a perfect example of the Black male using Coolposing methods to create long lasting change-Coltrane changed the face of Jazz music forever.

W.E.B. DuBois, who did the first scholarly study of Black males as business leaders, in his study of the Philadelphia Negro recognized that cool was present inside Black males back in 1899.

When positive Black male role models enter class rooms, lies and misconceptions are cleared up, and great learning occurs.
(Courier-Post)

Verbose Black males usually rise to leadership positions
because they can arouse the spirit of their followers
by speaking the power of the ancestors into existence.
(Marc & Evelyne Bernheim)

Through collectivism, the Black male can claim his leadership role
as the molder of young Black boys by providing rites
of passage into manhood.
(Marc & Evelyne Bernheim)

Coolposing father in harmony and accord
with his son through communicative individuality.
(Marc & Evelyne Bernheim)

Coolposing teacher in accord with students' needs and aspirations.
(Courier-Post)

The Disc Jockey (DJ) is one of the coolest images in America, with
vigor, accord, mysticism, collectivism, and above all, verboseness
(wordiness)-remember, the measure of a man is his mouth!
(Vincent Smith)

When Black males tell their story to their children, they also reveal
their style-once this happens, the pain ends and understanding begins.
(Courier-Post)

5

WHY BLACK MALES *BULLS**T* SO WELL

When many Europeans are in the company of people of color,
they are either consciously or subconsciously preoccupied
with the thought that there is nothing more important than
being White.

—James Baldwin (Writer)

Coolposing is a leadership strategy based on African cultural elements of communicative individuality and mysticism, emerging from influences of cool pose. It is a viable approach to stability and flexibility by providing remediation for any major mismatch between the nature of the job and the nature of the person who does the job. In job settings in which human values place a distant second behind economic ones, and burnout thrives, Coolposing, with its self-correcting personal alignment, gains ideological legitimacy across socioeconomic groups of Black males. Coolposing represents an important approach for Black male leaders to provide a positive response to negative organizational behavior.

Black male business decision-making and leadership styles have evolved from the African logic-system, and make plenty of sense to many Black Americans, despite how confusing it may be to the Westerner. Time and its management by Black males in business, is based on African social time, which is meaningful to conflicts in historical time. The difference between African-centered and Western-centered psychology is that the Westerner mainly has a problem-solving mind while the African primarily has a situation-experiencing mind. Thinking of a linear or a line of time in Western thought sees an infinite future, where African thinking sees the future as virtually absent because events in it have not taken place, they have not been realized, and cannot, therefore, be called "time".

Black males in business find stability and flexibility in the use of African personality theory-based leadership, which establishes the point that African social consciousness is neither superior nor inferior to any other but certainly different. Coolposing is filtered from African society and cannot be defined exclusively in terms of Western or Euro-American terminology, hence the expressive language, which some call "slang", "cool-speech" or "hip-hop vernacular", yet it is vital for the accuracy of the meaning. Those who see something more useful in existence frequently reject Western philosophies, such as capitalism and Christian doctrine that have been imposed on Africa and African descendants during slavery.

Many Black males use their mouths as the determination of their masculinity, creating the term "The measure of a man is his mouth". The term allows speaking or "rapping" to dominate over reading and writing as symbols of manhood. Bullshitting sessions (BS sessions), with exaggeration, talking about each other's families badly, and paying little attention to the truth, are major events in Black male rituals. Many of the most successful men in the BS sessions are poorly educated and do not have degrees or certificates of academic achievement. By contrast, not having at least a degree from a two-year college would leave these same men viewed as unsuccessful, poor wage earners based upon European standards.

The rejection of European ideas shows in the moving away from materialism by some Black males, who recognize Kwanzaa, for instance, as an African-centered, non-materialistic alternative to Christmas, and see that Egypt is to Africa as Greece is to Europe. Many Black males, raised in traditional American belief systems, now explore Islam, Buddhism, Hinduism, and even Atheism yet still hold the principles of African cultural based leadership in high regard. Communicative individualism and mysticism are culture-carrying traits that can be related to adult workers on the one hand, and explain the quickly changing cultural values of Black youth on the other hand. *Coolposing* allows the Black male to use expressive or *cool* performances to seek identity, strength and flexibility through African-centered philosophy-based leadership roles that sometimes use Western forms altered to suit their personal and group tastes.

Black males are strongly seeking freedom, empowerment and voice as leaders of businesses and searching for support systems to overcome socio-cultural obstacles in securing capital for business maintenance and increased patronage from Blacks and other groups. *Coolposing* is a strategy for values-based leadership, which promotes the rejection of media images of a cool pose culture, which primarily concern unemployed and troubled Black males. Black males want to make choices and decisions, use their ability to think and solve problems, and have input in the process of achieving the outcomes for which they will be held accountable-on their terms.

"It's a Black thing that you wouldn't understand" is a statement that takes on new meaning. Black males seek cultivation of a distinctive personality and spiritual satisfaction through values-based decision-making. More Black males than are reported in the media are economically secure, have family authority, provide well for their families, lead professional middle-class lives, avoid problems with the criminal justice system, maintain involvement in church and community, and extend their involvement to national issues. These less known Black males have the tendency for relatively high levels of motivation for action and an energetic approach to life. They are effective, as well as expressive, and reflect the most desirable image of decision-making and leadership style for Black male businessmen.

Coolposing leadership provides the means to achieve dynamic outcomes and focuses first, on exposing the fraudulent ways of seeing and being that suggests the history experienced by Black males does not belong to them, but perhaps they are owned by, and belong to it. Second, it reveals that Black males erroneously knew themselves only through their roles in the family, community, school, or city, and not as leaders capable of forging unlimited realities. Finally, *Coolposing* helps bring new awareness to Black males to approach each leadership decision as experts.

Coolposing, as a leadership strategy, provides the impetus to ensure that the Black male takes the responsibility for the socialization and the education of his family. He is also forced to recognize that if his children are to be saved in the full sense of the word, then, he must become involved in pursuing the complete Cultural Revolution in the business community necessary for their salvation. The Black male, within the *Coolposing* philosophy, is instructed how to educate and socialize his children for *mastery* and *control*, to be the best among all people and not minimum wage earners. Most importantly, Black males in leadership roles are encouraged to not perpetuate negative behaviors of the past, such as irresponsible parenting, husbanding, and friendship, which will help to change the face of American society forever.

Coolposing basically says "To hell with societal norms dictating masculine performance as generally White male specific!" and acknowledge those unable to gain materialism, prestige, personal possessions and wealth as being as capable as any other, since masculinity and manhood are not the property of a select group. Through adapting a type of behavior management innovation such as *Coolposing*, and embracing the processes and policies that are related to them, many Black male leaders will avoid personal anxiety, psychological disorder, and depression associated with exclusion and discrimination. Essentially, *Coolposing* is a positive response to stress, and a contributor to freedom, empowerment and voice.

It is important to focus on the deeper meaning of *Coolposing* to reduce future confusion regarding this dynamic approach to Black male leadership. Black male businessmen most often take in more profit than hourly wage earners, which firmly places them in the middle class or "black bourgeoisie", which historically have been the most schizoid of all Black groups. The schizoid Black maintains a love-hate relation to himself, his people, and other peoples (particularly Whites). His life is characterized by a constant movement between two conflicting worlds of differing histories, lifestyles, values and more.

The Black male who belongs to the middle class has no fixed reference point, which he can use with confidence to guide his life, values, goals, attitudes, and behaviors, and to stabilize his relations to himself as well as others. As a result, his relations with himself and others are confused even though these may be smoothed over by a phony harmony. What is significant is that the middle class, Black or White, is particularly adept at maintaining fronts, which is the foundation of coolposing. The only thing separating the middle class Black male from the ghetto-dwelling Black male is money; they both fail to establish consistent limits, which their children can readily and easily comprehend to guide their current and future behavior. The child, in an effort to adapt to the behavior of his schizoid parent(s) begins to develop a confused, powerless, contradictory, emotionally crippled, incompetent, retarded, and schizoid personality like that of his parent(s).

COOLPOSING

Given the Afro-centric outlook that helps many Blacks assert themselves: "I am because we are; and since we are, therefore I am", values emphasizing mutual respect, family, community, and nation are highly valued. Since Afro-centrism is a collective philosophy connected to meaningful cultural traditions and institutions—leadership style will have to reflect the nine kinds of cool of the total group value of *mysticism, accord, flexibility, vigor, change agency, collectivism, communicative individuality, verboseness, and shared-time perspective*. The Afro-centric idea, which is group-focused, attempts to socialize children toward values that elevate the interests of the community over the individual. In other words, you cannot be a drug dealer and be respected in an Afro-centric community. The only communities that will respect drug dealers are those that value money over people, and they are all soon destroyed from within, usually by drug dealers.

Historically, native-born Africans viewed themselves in the context of family and social obligations to community. Leadership must be viewed from an Afro-centric group perspective. If you are wealthy and hurting your people then you are *worthless*.

Coolposing confuses and baffles those that hope to do psychological damage to Black males. Cool is really a black thing that many do not understand because in coolness is a search for life's meaning, or at least America's meaning; once the *why* is discovered, the Black male endures any, *how*. Inside leadership-cool, is a form of freedom, empowerment and voice that Black men seek for stability and flexibility in harmony with their cosmic world-view. The freedom is self-generating, the empowerment also replenishes itself and the voice resonates forever in the life force of cool. Following is an application of the strategy of *Coolposing:*

Cross Theory of Ethnic Identity (CTEI)

In order to gain an in-depth understanding of Black male leadership in America, it is significant to understand how ethnic identity develops and the process that occurs to achieve balance with one's self. The following theory is how individuals become who they were destined to be.

1. **What were you told?** Did the information generated about your existence make sense to you or were there areas of question that left you wondering and seeking more? If there was a degree of nonsense involved, then you are not congruent or balanced. (Heard-Received)

2. **What did you behold?** Did your experiences confirm or deny the information generated about your existence? For instance, was the information acceptable or unacceptable? If there was a significant amount of contradiction to the information, such as being told you had no vital history then discovering that your ancestors figured prominently in global developments, you are not congruent or balanced. (Saw-Believed)

3. **What should unfold?** Can you think of a desired life for yourself that will please you and is obtainable? If the life you imagine is unexpected, then stop here, however if the life you imagine is expected, then you have succeeded in reaching the awareness needed for congruency and balance. (Wondered-Conceived)

Congruence, balance and love of self is the goal of ethnic identity

Innovative Information: Verbal communication must increase in its intensity with the utilization of more complex and challenging vocabulary to advance knowledge of self (epistemology).

Innovative Reformation: Lived experience must increase in its quality with more phenomenological exploration or questioning of each nuance with why, when, where, who, how, and what of self (axiology).

Innovative Transformation: Warranted spiritual shift must occur to assist in restructuring a world-view of congruence, balance, and love of self and one's people with respect for all others (cosmology).

Dr. George Cross, DM: Congruence entails balancing deficits and resources of contrasting views.
[*A mechanistic view inevitably generates an organic contrast whose contact produces a congruent idea by harmonizing deficits and resources.* see *CROSS COOL POSING CONNECTION STRATEGY* ©]

Related theories of development:

George Hegel: In order to understand any aspect of human culture, we must retrace and understand its history [*history* driven].

Lev Vygotsky: Healthy growth relies on the importance of culture, central role of language and zone of proximal development [*culture* driven].

Albert Bandura: Human behavior is learned observationally through attention, retention, motor production, and motivation [*environment* driven].

Jean Piaget: Social interaction is the primary source of cognition and behavior [*society* driven].

Victor Frankl: If a person is shown a *why*, they will conceive any *how* [*meaning* driven].

MECHANISTIC CURRICULUM [Thesis]	CONGRUENCE [Synthesis]	COOL POSING LEARNERS [Antithesis]
Materialism	Aspirations	Spirituality
Impulse Control	Discipline	Movement
Separateness	Skill	Expressiveness
Reason	Knowledge	Emotion
Individualism	Empathy	Communalism
Mastery of Nature	Style	Harmony
Possessiveness	Design	Verve
Literacy	Story	Orality
Clock Time	Meaning	Personal Time

CROSS COOL POSING CONNECTION STRATEGY ©
[Curriculum Intervention]

Interventions are designed to reduce tension, frustration, confusion, and hurt that often gets in the way of successful implementation of teaching and learning. Essentially, the thesis and the antithesis must be brought into synthesis with a new concept: that concept is Cross Cool Posing Connection Strategy.

6

WHY BLACK MALES ARE
LATE A WHOLE LOT

*These brothers are so tardy their names are prefaced with
"The late . . ." while they are still alive.*

—[Anonymous]

The huge majority of African-descended people living in the United States before the Civil War were slaves. Consequently, even free Black males had little choice for whom and under what circumstances they would work. Labor income accounts for a majority of the racial wealth gap. The massive wealth differences between Blacks and Whites directly links to the enormous inequality in the labor income of both. Black males relied on cool behaviors with more frequency than other groups to cope with their stress from more harsh socioeconomic conditions than other groups. Because of their need to use cunning and craftiness to survive, one result of the cruel conditions realized by Black males was their great difficulty of abiding by the racist laws and the resulting criminality.

The legal system preyed on Black men to fill its prisons to keep wardens and guards employed, as well as bolster the available hirable help for local industry, such as the timber growers and cotton planters. Many Black males, some only children, were locked up on mostly bogus and petty charges in wholesale sweeps, and then made available to cotton planters, railroad operators, road builders and other employers to be used as they wished. These employers worked the Black males harder than slaves had been, often starved them, and gave them the worst shelter and clothing. There was no healthcare-if a prisoner got sick or died accidentally, there was little concern over the loss because there were more where he came from.

Convict leasing of the South was a cash arrangement between the police and plantation owners that allowed the forced labor of former slaves convicted of crimes such as vagrancy, and is an inherited legacy of Black males. Laws passed to keep Blacks and especially Black males as slaves reveal the scheme to keep them as the permanent underclass in America. From 1808 to 1854, the Georgia General Assembly passed laws against the manumission or freeing of slaves. South Carolina required that free Blacks pay a special tax for the privilege of being Black and maintain residence in the state. Failure to pay the tax resulted in a fine or imprisonment, which led to leasing him out for a period necessary to satisfy the fine.

If a free Black person were twice guilty of helping a slave run away, then return to bondage was the consequence for him. An incentive to remove free Blacks from society provided that the white person bringing charges of corruption could collect half of the proceeds from the newly enslaved Black. In addition, free Blacks in Georgia had to work on public projects when they were made to appear necessary by local justices of the Inferior

Court for a period of up to twenty days per year. Unfair punishment such as this added greatly to Georgia's treasury and served the key objective of keeping Black males in their place.

The profitability of convict leasing encouraged the criminalizing of Black males of an ever-larger number of offenses. The post-Civil War plantation economy, in order to restore the social situation thought by Whites to be best for Blacks, closely resembled slavery. The isolation of Blacks from African culture since the slavery era and isolation of Blacks from Whites in America generated unique verbal and nonverbal behaviors that contributed to coolness.

We have never stopped being Africans;
Speaking, minus our tongues,
With the drums of mental telepathy;
Planting, minus our whole seed,
The flowering cuttings of tribal-ness;
Wanting, minus hills and rivers that know us,
A land once more
Of leopard's boldness and lion's pride.
We have never stopped wearing the life masks of ancestors
Who, through us, gaze over all human time.
For a long while we have brewed in our heart memory's herbs,
Prepared the drink of peoplehood.
We have never stopped being what we have preserved.
And now we flourish.

—Sharon Bourke

Legal regulations, known as the *Black Codes* maintained the legitimacy of slavery, thus recognizing Black people as property, and guaranteeing property owner rights. Although many police, sheriffs, property owners and plantation overseers treated Black people as non-humans, extensive legislation restricted them, which clearly demonstrated the knowledge or fear of many others that Black people were indeed human, deprived of schooling and intentionally kept ignorant and subservient. The constant threat of violence in the antebellum South forced Black people, and primarily Black men, to display an ignorance that was not genuine, but required for survival. This coping mechanism helped save them from beatings and lynching by remaining cool in crisis.

Free Blacks were free only in the most limited way and under no circumstances was he to be a citizen. No matter what the free Black did, he could never legally rise above the status of a denizen, which was not an alien nor citizen. Any person having one drop of so-called "Negro blood" was considered Black, yet the reverse was not true; no matter how much so-called "Caucasian blood" a Black had, he was always Black-the offspring of an interracial pairing was only Black.

In contrast to published records indicating disharmony, evidence collected through unique interviews of Black males in America ranging from those once enslaved to those prospering in the 21st century reveal the camaraderie of the group. Black males were not as docile as the erroneously historical depiction of them suggests. Slave owners and corporate executives both attempted to publicly treat the Black male as if he were a joke, a pathetic creature, or a thing to be cared for, all the while secretly admiring and envying him in a homoerotic manner. Significant incidents have occurred throughout history that support the idea that the dominant European society, especially White males, which mandated the behavior that was seen as "acceptable" by Black males, suffered from an *attraction-repulsion syndrome*. In this unique condition, White America's general state involves their admiration of the creative genius of Black males in athletics, entertainment and the arts, and at the same time considers in disgust his skin color, potency to cause genetic annihilation and unmatchable coolness.

These sordid details of the Black male's past that disregarded any and all plans for a timely future have left an indelible print on his psyche regarding clock time. When he was incarcerated he was doing time, when he was released he was making up for lost time, when he was unemployed he was wasting time, when he was involved in work he was clocking time, and all the while, because of huge gaps in his quality time, time was passing him by. The African logic system of time shows a past where events and emotions reside, which gives it priority over a future where nothing has happened yet. Part of the concept of "CP" (Coolposing) time is that lateness is most likely caused because there was an experience that was too energetic to leave in a timely manner.

Since many Black males have a situation experiencing orientation to life ("What's happening?" "Did you hear the latest?" "What it is?"), they tend to have situation experiencing minds, which are not necessarily concerned with immediate problem solving. It is a common sight to see Black males on the way to school, and on time, then see a situation occur that will make them seriously late. What was it that he found too irresistible to wait until later to discover the outcome of the situation? The short answer is that the answer to the problem is not as interesting as the situation itself.

The development of a problem solving perspective or way of thinking has to become the goal of Black males who seek success in America. America is a country whose business is business, therefore in order to be relevant in America one must learn how to effectively take care of business and essentially the most successful businesses are the ones that solve its problems best. Its employees have problem-solving minds, which require timely arrival, productive engagement, and often late departures from the workplace.

A good exercise for Black males, young and old is to recite the words written by Nathan Hare, Ph.D., titled "I am a Black man":

> "The evidence of anthropology now suggests that I, the Black man, am the original man, the first man to walk this vast imponderable earth. I, the Black man, am an African, the exotic quintessence of a universal blackness. I have lost by force my land, my language, in a sense my life, I will seize it back so help me.
>
> Toward that end, if necessary, I will crush the corners of the earth, and this world will surely tremble, until I, the Black man, the first and original man, can arm in arm with my woman, erect among the peoples of the universe a new society, humane to its cultural core, out of which at long last will emerge, as night moves into day, the first truly human being that the world has ever known."

7

WHY GANGS MATTER SO MUCH TO SOME BLACK MALES

I fought with fists and lost them all,
some to the great and some to the small.

—Dr. George Cross, DM

Gangs are like families to many Black males who have been denied a functional two-parent, gainfully employed, and resource producing one. Given the high rate of divorce and separation among Black families stemming from lack of finances and related support mechanisms, the means of gaining valuable resources often lead to decisions to join gangs. Most street gangs provide protection and psychological support for its members, even though lawbreaking activities and recklessness are included in the equation. The key attraction to the gang lifestyle for many Black males is the belief of a connection to manhood by being involved in coolposing activities that bring attention and renown, although often short-lived.

Historically, southern Black males relied on groups to escort them along deserted roads that served as routes for the Ku Klux Klan looking to catch one or more unsuspecting victims. The larger the group of Black males, however the less likely the Klansmen would risk a confrontation with them; especially, since the group was usually armed. The protection that the group provided was not only life-saving it was life-changing, and enriching. The trip to the appointed destination was filled with conversation, laughter, information, and play. These bonding rituals extend from an African heritage and are difficult to simply drop.

After the Great Black Migration of the 1920s through the 1950s that saw millions leave the segregated and impoverished south for the slightly integrated and industrialized north, gangs were no longer necessary-no longer needed for their initial purpose of protection against the Klan, that is. Since old habits often die hard, many transplanted southerners who settled in the same neighborhoods, continued with the rituals of gathering in groups. Soon, there began the tradition of naming the group by neighborhood or street intersection, such as "23rd and Diamond Street" or "The Valley". Bragging rights were connected to conquering a rival gang, which ushered in the gang war era. Gang war death tolls equaled that of real wars in small countries, yet the fixation to the gangs has not wavered significantly in decades.

An eerie honor is actually bestowed upon survivors of gang wars, who are referred to as "gang bangers". They get attention when they enter a room and others speak their name with a sense of awe, such as, "That brother over there has more bodies than most soldiers. Don't get in his way", with *bodies* referring to murders. He will walk the streets free because the gangs have a "no snitching" policy that allows them to terrorize neighborhoods with no clear consequence. Of course, they eventually get *theirs* however it usually comes long after they have done more than their share of damage to the neighborhood and its residents.

So, why are so many Black males still attracted to gangs after seeing the death and destruction that they cause and recognizing the immediate danger that exists for them upon joining? Working with probation officers and social workers for the past ten years in a volatile urban city, it is clear that the increasing lack of education required to land significant jobs is a key reason. With few or no marketable skills and little preparation for a highly technical workplace, many Black males are afraid to compete against better prepared individuals for hard to get jobs. In place of working to better ones self, many take the so-called short-cut to money and resources through gang involvement, not knowing that most short-cuts are cut short.

Gangs provide some conveniences such as girls, drugs, weapons, notoriety, access to food, shelter and clothing, and cash. Inconveniences are also provided such as injuries, incarceration, and death. A desperate person with no sense of the future could easily select the temporary conveniences over the longer-lasting inconveniences, which may account for the steady stream of recruits to gangland. While gang rituals can be traced to West African culture, which extended to America, the reasons for the American rituals are certainly disconnected from those of West Africa by more than the length of the Atlantic Ocean.

The West African groupings by age were a major part of the initiation rites in the preparation of the boy for manhood. The age group provided a balanced development for African youth who were competing with those of the same size, weight, height, and experience. The tasks to be completed were designed by the elders of the village and they allowed the boys to show resourcefulness and responsibility, which were key aspects of manhood. A task may have involved the capturing of a wild animal with weapons that required great skill and cunning. Another task may have been placing the male in an intimate arrangement with a female which required the male to show restraint in his passionate desires. The ability to hold off ones desires until the right time is a key part of manhood.

Today, the lack of adult involvement in their communities, which are the modern day villages, leaves an empty hole for the rituals to manhood of long ago. Add this to the overall neglect and fear shown by many parents of properly raising their sons, and the boy is going to fall back on the dysfunctional guidance of his peer group, who also suffer from neglect.

The misinformed peer group sets the standards and the guidelines of their behavior and along the way create strange and ignorant requirements for reaching manhood. Perhaps because of the parental neglect, and anger, much of the peer group and gangs' rituals for manhood are in direct opposition of the mother and father's authority.

Gang membership shows the Black male that he is cool as he rebels against feminine authority such as his mother, babysitters, elementary and secondary school teachers, and even girls. With girls he is confused because while he desires them biologically for sex and affection, he rejects them socially as part of his masculine protest in which he seeks to establish his masculine identity therefore he will call them "bitches" while still seeking their acceptance.

Since many gang members come from homes that are disorganized because of poverty where permissiveness and lack of parental supervision is common, they grow up basically unparented. They have no clear picture of parenting, which consists of planned meals, set bedtimes, activities, and structured rules. It is easy for them to make up bits and pieces of how life should be based on what they heard, read, or saw someone else do rather than relate to their own experiences. Overall, so much has been lost in the developmental lives of gang members because of the lack of discipline, empathy, rules, responsibilities, and respect that it is not uncommon to see gangs of youth acting as neighborhood terrorists with no regard to consequences.

An immediate danger of gang membership, outside of injury, incarceration, and death, is recognizing that their authority figures shift from parents and teachers to police, courts, social workers, foster homes, counselors, probation officers, and psychologists trying to help figure out what is wrong with them. An added danger is that the gang member, who seeks manhood, actually experiences the opposite; he engages in an extended boyhood because so many adult authority figures have legal rights to advise, counsel, mediate, arrest, and hold him against his will. This is the total opposite of the freedom sought through manhood.

The contradiction of seeking a short-cut to manhood only to receive an extended, and smothering childhood, causes trauma to the young Black male. He rebels against his situation, which is self-inflicted, but does not take the blame; he passes blame on to his absent parents. Even though he knows he is lying to himself, he tells the lie to social workers and psychologists, who need him as a client, therefore they "say" they believe him and begin to provide the state-funded counseling services that will make him whole again. Without elaborating further on this scenario, a change must be made in the system of bringing young Black males involved in gang activity to manhood.

An obvious error in many gang members' ideas of manhood is physical prowess. There are entirely too many young Black males viewing jail as a rite of passage to manhood that establishes them as having conquered a great feat. A common sight in many communities is seeing a returning convict, built like a football player from lifting weights in the exercise yard and not books in the library, gain the attention of other young men who anxiously await hearing of the great adventure he just experienced.

The returning convict usually will not disappoint his audience by telling them about the fights, the bullying, the "fun", and the manhood. The wide-eyed youth many times envision themselves behind bars participating in the events. What is left out of the one-sided tale is the homosexuality, fear, abuse, deception, psychological damage, retardation of potential, anxiety, moral decline, family disconnect, theft of childhood, destructive intention, hopelessness, loss of education, and suicidal tendencies.

The breakdown in the African American communities which produce the coolposing Black males can only be salvaged through a return to customs, traditions, ceremonies, and rituals which have provided the means for survival for Africans through the beginning of time to now. The neglected African traditions of spirituality, orality, personal time, harmony, emotion, communalism, movement, verve, and affect have to be reintroduced into the lives of the Black male at home, school, and the work place. Manhood in African culture involved commitment and responsibility to family, women and children, and not a gang, showing irresponsibility, non-commitment and disrespect to family, women and children.

We can begin to break up the gang by destroying the need for gangs. Gangs do not exist where responsible and committed young men exist. A young Black male who holds his mother, father, and family in the highest regard can never be duped into joining a gang by a group of his peers. First of all, he would recognize that the group is most likely jealous of the stable family the young man enjoys and would like nothing better than to see him live in the sorry conditions in which they reside. Most gang members have experienced lives of less than adequate love and affection. Education can provide alternatives to walking around feeling sorry for themselves-it can provide ways to build from the failed situation and grow. It is never too late for anyone, especially Black males to be what they could have been despite bad beginnings. Most importantly, Black males have to be better understood by America, and that can best begin with school teachers.

8

WHY IT IS UP TO TEACHERS TO BETTER UNDERSTAND BLACK MALES

Black male students have been doing wrong for so long that doing right seems wrong.

—Dr. George Cross, DM

I have examined the phenomenon of "Coolposing" through description, narration, exposition, and persuasion, however the purpose of this book is to further provide ways that America can truly understand the Black male as a leader. To accomplish this difficult task, old perceptions of westernized leadership must be challenged, which includes authoritarian, democratic, collaborative, and lassez faire, among others. In the 21st millennium, where deceptive financial practices have occurred at mind-boggling rates at the highest levels (think Enron, Bernie Maddoff, Wall Street), Black males have never figured prominently in them. More than racism and bias hiring practices, which kept them out, history shows that their leadership style, grounded in African-based morals would have generally prevented them from engaging in the sinfulness of cheating their friends and families on the grand scale of the westerner. Ancestral commitment, which is a rarely discussed value, is very much alive among the business and leadership practices of many Black males.

The dilemma faced by Black males in the 2000s is formed by historical, social, and cultural elements that have generated a negative bias that must be correctly contradicted in order to provide more accurate and positive models of Black males. This chapter suggests methods that may trigger policy changes and viewpoints that can improve the political, educational, legal, health, and business conditions in which Black males in America thrive.

The following poem is an historical overview of the Black males' journey in North America. I focused on the theme of being the group that specifically entered America to work and ironically find itself as the group that America's employers are most against. Teachers in various content areas can find a way to utilize the poem's content to aid theirs. History and Social Studies may be the easiest to implement, while English Language Arts can find the literary terms of simile and metaphor useful. Science teachers can identify the agricultural technology and math teachers can construct timelines that can be coordinated with other content areas. Music, Dance, and Drama teachers can collaborate on a production that can include Art and Poetry. This is merely one possibility of reaching out to the "too cool for school" generation in the context of delivering a mechanistic and mandated curriculum that receives serious student resistance.

We were brought here to work . . .
Now, we can't find a job!
We left rich spacious land
Under full velvet skies
Eating food grown by hand
Watched by ancestors' eyes
Snaring fish from the sea
Chasing lions on land
Sharing shade from a tree
With a woman or man
Then, to leave that behind
Forces a strong heart to sob
We were brought here to work
Now we can't find a job

We were creating new worlds
Without spending a dime
Whenever problems unfurled
We simply solved them in time
There were very few things
That our teachers would fear
So they passed on to kings
Who whispered in the queen's ear
Oh, we had riches and gold
And no reason to rob
We were brought here to work
Now we can't find a job

We danced to the drum
After working the fields
The singers would hum
Praising bountiful yields
The young virgins were ripe
For the warriors' touch
But, the village was hyped
Against the actions of such
We ate the fresh corn

And discarded the cob
We were brought here to work
Now we can't find a job

Now, we struggle for crumbs
As we're pushed to the side
We are shoved into slums
And some folks don't care who died
All we have left is will
Although some fools still brag
That they'll rob and they'll kill
For a jive nickel bag
And descendants of God
Now, belong to the mob
We were brought here to work
Now, we can't find a job?

—*George Cross III, DM, 2009©*

SCHOOLS AND BLACK MALES

"Get out of my face!"

"Young man, all I asked you to do was to take off your hoodie and have a seat."

"Y'all teachers always telling somebody something, like you so smart."

"You have a choice; hoodie off and sit down or hoodie on and get out."

"See, there you go, always trying to kick somebody out."

"The school has rules. No hoodies."

"Look at your clothes."

"I am not violating a school rule, you are."

"You know what? I don't need this. I am out of here."

"Bye."

One of the major places of conflict and crisis for Black males is school. The apparent mismatch between the perception of Black males by administrators and teachers, and their reality causes them to be pushed out of school at a rate that is twice that of other groups. Much of the misunderstanding comes from the inability of educators to correctly read the cultural behaviors of Black males that include strutting or strolling, rapping, jonning or wolfing, playing the dozens or sounding, using slang, wearing expressive clothing like sagging pants, loose hoodies, and do-rags, or other artifacts that they view as cool.

Since schools operate from the cultural norms of the middle class, with its suburban values in dress, mannerisms, language, ethics, and etiquette, individuals who were never shown these norms or hidden rules are obvious victims of violating them. For example, a young Black male may smile or smirk while being reprimanded by a teacher or school administrator as a way of showing coolness or hyper-masculinity which he learned among his peers, unaware of the middle class norm where a reprimand is serious and should be experienced with shame and forgiveness. The young man in this scenario may have to actually have the rules of reprimand explained to him, despite how obvious they may appear to others.

If the reprimanded young man is from a family where poverty is common and gainful employment is lacking, who is going to teach him the rules of the middle class? His parents may not have learned the middle class norms because of the lack of their exposure in the workplace, where norms are usually learned. Most schools have no course in middle class norms-they are expected to be known. The problem for Black males is that the middle class norms are learned in middle class homes, where they have little or no access. When teachers see students from lower income areas displaying behavior that opposes the school endorsed middle class norms, they say things such as "Stop that, and act right!", "What is wrong with you? Don't you know how to act?", "You know better than that!", or "I know you were not raised like that!" In each case the educator could be wrong.

Teachers can begin the difficult work toward better understanding Black males in America by asking themselves, "How does 'Coolposing' look in the classroom?" This question opens up a positive area for exploration and can enable new ways of viewing the same thing. The two lists below were constructed from research on the behavioral traits identified with Coolposing. The first list views Coolposing behaviors from a deficit or negative perspective, and the second list views the identical behavior from a resource, useful, and positive, workable perspective:

From a [**DEFICIT**] perspective, Coolposing will appear as the following:

1. ACTING OUT
2. ETHNIC HUMOR
3. ROLES
4. SHIELDS
5. SELF-EXPRESSION
6. SOCIAL FRONTS
7. FEARLESS
8. STRUCTURING OF PSYCHE
9. RITUALS
10. WALKS-STROLL
11. FACADES
12. INVERSION
13. UNIQUE POSES
14. POSTURES
15. ESTABLISHED PERFORMANCES
16. COPING MECHANISMS
17. SHUCKING
18. PSYCHOLOGICAL DEFENSES
19. INTENTIONS
20. DETACHED
21. COMPULSIVE MASCULINITY
22. TOUGH
23. SURVIVAL MECHANISMS
24. COMPENSATORY DEVICES
25. CREATIVE SPEECH
26. EXPRESSIVE GESTURES
27. AUTHENTIC HAIR STYLES/CLOTHING
28. THREATENING AND PURPOSEFUL STANCES
29. STRATEGIC DEMEANOR
30. EMOTIONLESS

However, from a [**RESOURCE**] perspective, Coolposing in the classroom can blossom into the following:

1. ACTING OUT (drama, playwright, helper, messenger)
2. ETHNIC HUMOR (stand-up comedy, comedy writing, M.C.)
3. ROLES (negotiator, acting, role play director)
4. SHIELDS (safety patrol, science investigator)
5. SELF-EXPRESSION (painter, artist, actor)
6. SOCIAL FRONTS (hotel-restaurant-travel major)
7. FEARLESS (sports-football, technology, problem solver)
8. STRUCTURING OF PSYCHE (social work, administration)
9. RITUALS (historian, cultural arts, rules committee, clergy)
10. WALKS-STROLL (hall monitor, mail carrier UPS, FedEx)
11. FACADES (acting, novelist, magician, illusionist)
12. INVERSION (creative writing, puzzle maker)
13. UNIQUE POSES (modeling, photography, realtor)
14. POSTURES (business major, network marketer)
15. ESTABLISHED PERFORMANCES (performance artist)
16. COPING MECHANISMS (resilience, job survivor, cop)
17. SHUCKING (debater, class spokesperson, car dealer)
18. PSYCHOLOGICAL DEFENSES (law, business, counselor)
19. INTENTIONS (planning, goal setting, advising)
20. DETACHED (study skills, focused reader, casino dealer)
21. COMPULSIVE MASCULINITY (sports, sports reporting)
22. TOUGH (army, law officer, security, collector, repo man)
23. SURVIVAL MECHANISMS (workplace, college, street)
24. COMPENSATORY DEVICES (leadership, businessman)
25. CREATIVE SPEECH (debate, orator, politician)
26. EXPRESSIVE GESTURES (theater, drama, musician)
27. AUTHENTIC HAIR STYLES/CLOTHING (design/stylist)
28. THREATENING AND PURPOSEFUL STANCES (guard)
29. STRATEGIC DEMEANOR (chess player, problem solver)
30. EMOTIONLESS (bomb squad, SWAT team, K-9 corps)

The two lists show a startling example of what can occur once old ways of *seeing* are replaced with new ways of *being*. The desire for Black males in school is for movement and not the static method that the current school curriculum is presented. Males prefer more activity in learning-their physiques even indicate this. Teachers have to recognize how often during a teacher-directed lecture they see students (primarily males) fidgeting. The movement is not an indication that the lecture is boring, it is a clear sign that these students need more stimulation in their learning, and if they do not get it, they may begin to act-out, so they can at least witness movement as they are escorted to the principal or disciplinarian's office.

In classes where there are males and females, teachers may schedule one long activity of 40 minutes or more that females tend to excel, then on another day select several short activities of 10-15 minutes that males tend to desire. The research on males is available yet not read-males require movement, enjoy noise, have shorter attention spans, seek competitive engagement, and like to have clear "winners" and "losers" in activities. Teachers can help themselves tremendously by implementing these strategies.

When conferencing with males teachers commit a major error by placing the male in a chair or at a table directly across from them. That is not how males talk during their leisure time; they talk to each other from the side. Watch males play sports, such as football and basketball; they give each other orders and ideas from the side as they line up for the next play. Observe males walking down the street or standing around on a playground; they talk to each other from the side and glance at each other's faces occasionally, without staring. Staring is what the females tend to do, which makes many males slightly uncomfortable ("What is she looking for?" "Is my face all right?" "Is there something green on my teeth?"). Teachers may find more success in simply talking to a male student at a casual moment such as on the bleachers during gym, on the cafeteria long benches, or in the media center, with chairs arranged side by side instead of directly across from each other.

THE ROLE OF THE TEACHER

Teachers are the bridge between the visionary ideals of administration and the chaotic reality of students. They must synthesize the desires of students and administration and incorporate it into new knowledge. Since the environment of teaching and learning is continuously in flux, so must the nature of knowledge. The school and university acting on the environment not only perform effective information processing but also creates information and knowledge by itself. This process involves not merely a strategy of reducing the information-processing burden; it also requires the school and university to evolve itself by amplifying its own diversity, destroying the existing patterns of thought and behavior, and creating new patterns. After all, it is through the development of shared meaning and understanding that the cycles of structured behaviors themselves become sensible and meaningful.

The phenomenon of students' "Coolposing" or engaging in street-related actions that maintain their self-esteem independent of how badly they are doing in school, is an environmental issue that demands the school and university's attention. Coolposing is seen as hanging out on the street after school, shopping and dressing sharply, sexual conquests, party drugs, excessive listening to hip-hop music, emulating superstar athletes and entertainers on school grounds, and intentional under performance in school. The failure to identify with academic achievement as being essential to their self-esteem creates the paradox that new and veteran teachers must examine. Coolposing provides a vehicle for immediate gratification and frequently gains a great deal of respect from other youths, regardless of race. A puzzling finding by social psychologists is that young black males and females tend to have the highest levels of self-esteem of all ethnic groups while achieving among the poorest academically of all ethnic groups.

The challenge for schools and universities is to explore Coolposing as a new and temporary culture that has engulfed many youths, particularly young Black men. School administrators and educators have to identify the contradictions, such as the more involved youths become in Coolposing the more disconnected from the socioeconomic mainstream they become. In other words, the cooler they become the poorer they get.

Even if there were attempts to discuss the selective engagement in Coolposing, such as when to turn off the hip-hop and pick up the SAT prep book it would serve as a starting point to the long needed discussion. English teachers and creative writing instructors may find value in assigning activities that lead to collecting transcripts of the Coolposers' views and rationalizations. One thing seems clear; the social scientists have exhausted their reasons for the strange behavior and the only group left to provide any sense making at all is the group that currently intentionally creates the confusion: Black males both mature and youthful.

HOW TEACHING ENGLISH LITERARY TERMS IS MADE COOL

The following literary terms are standard in any secondary English course. Knowing their definitions is essential for success. Memorizing these words requires much studying and practice. One of the greatest complaints of English Language Arts students is that there are so many rules and definitions that need to be learned that they interfere with the actual literature lesson that is of primary importance. Unfortunately, many English teachers use a method of teaching that burdens students with double-thinking, which is first they must think about the definition then they must place the definition in its proper place in the essay, report, poem, or composition. The following list of traditional literary terms challenges students to define each and quickly recall them when required:

1. IRONY—
2. MYTH—
3. PLOT—
4. RHYME—
5. TONE—
6. THEME—
7. TRAGEDY—
8. SYMBOL—
9. STYLE—
10. STANZA—
11. SPEAKER—
12. SONNET—
13. SIMILE—
14. SETTING—
15. RHYTHM—
16. POETRY—
17. COMEDY—
18. DRAMA—
19. ESSAY—
20. IDIOM—
21. HYPERBOLE—
22. METAPHOR—
23. METER—
24. ALLITERATION—

25. CONFLICT—
26. VOICE—
27. SUSPENSE—
28. FABLE—
29. ALLUSION—
30. PROVERB—
31. OXYMORON—
32. TRICKSTER—
33. NOVEL—
34. NARRATOR—
35. FICTION—
36. NONFICTION—
37. OCTAVE—
38. ONOMATOPOEIA—
39. PARADOX—
40. MINSTREL SHOW—
41. FOLK TALE—

It is clear that the list alone will require an enormous amount of study time and significant practice to keep the definitions fresh and clear in students' minds. It is not difficult to see why "cool" students dread attending English classes. The following list will show all of the literary terms from the first list and include fifty percent more terms, however a student will be able to recall the entire second list 500 percent faster than the first list because the second list is tailored to the cool students' learning style.

CROSS COOL POSING CURRICULUM©

The following literary terms, which are essential to know for success in school, are organized in a Coolposing manner that increases retention, understanding, and usefulness for future academic assignments. Notice the meanings of the terms are encased within the definitions so that the word actually "tells" its meaning.

42. IRONY—It Reverses ON You
43. MYTH—Makes You Think it Happened
44. PLOT—Play Lives On This

45. RHYME—Really Helps You Memorize Easier
46. TONE—'Tude Of Nearly Everything
47. THEME—The Heaviest Element that Meets the Eyes/Ears
48. TRAGEDY—The Raw Anger Growing Every Day in You
49. SYMBOL—Shows You Many Bits Of Life
50. STYLE—Shouts That Your Life's Extraordinary
51. STANZA—Stops To Allow New Zingers to Appear
52. SPEAKER—Single Person Explains All Kinds of Epic Realities
53. SONNET—Scheme Of Nice or Nasty Elegant Talking
54. SIMILE—Speech Intended to Make Imaginary Likeness Easy
55. SETTING—Shows Every Thing That Is Needed for Genesis
56. RHYTHM—Richly Helps You To Handle Movement
57. POETRY—Peace Of Experiencing The Real You
58. COMEDY—Clown On Most Every Day of the Year
59. DRAMA—Displays Real And Meaningful Action
60. ESSAY—Examines Serious Stories Around You
61. IDIOM—It Deals In Other Meanings
62. HYPERBOLE—Helps You Pick out Each Raw Bunch Of Lies and Exaggerations
63. METAPHOR—Makes Every Thing Appear Perfectly Harmonious Or Right
64. METER—Makes Every Thing End Right
65. ALLITERATION—ALL IT Ever Repeats Are Those Intense Or Noisy (consonants)
66. CONFLICT—Clash Of Numerous Forces Locked In Constant Turmoil
67. VOICE—Very Original Instrument Communicates Experiences
68. SUSPENSE—Slows Up Some Plots Especially Near Scary Endings
69. FABLE—Fast And Brief Lessons that Educate
70. ALLUSION—ALL of US Indirectly Omit Names
71. PROVERB—Proven Rules Of Values Enforcing the Right Behavior
72. OXYMORON—Only X-rays Your Mysterious Odd Recall Of Nonsense
73. TRICKSTER—This Rogue Is Cunning Keeps Skillful Tricks for Each Rival
74. NOVEL—New Original Vivid Element of Literature

75. NARRATOR—News Anchor Regularly Reports All Thoughts Or Reasons
76. FICTION—Fact Is Changed To Imagine Our Needs
77. NONFICTION—NO-Nonsense Fact Is Clear To Inform Our News
78. OCTAVE—Only Count The Actual Value of Eight
79. ONOMATOPOEIA—Orchestrated Nouns Or Musical Adjectives That Openly Provide Our Ears Instrumentals Aloud
80. PARADOX—People Are Rude Arrogant Dangerous Or Xenophobic
81. MINSTREL SHOW—Most Included Negro Slaves Traditional Routines and Expressive Lives—Stereotypes Hurt Original Works
82. FOLK TALE—Fable Or Legend Kept Told And Lives Endlessly
83. ALLEGORY—ALL Events Give Other Reasons to You
84. AMBIGUITY—Always Misleading Because It Gives Unclear Info To You
85. ANALOGY—A Noticeable Accurate Likeness Of Grownups and Youth
86. ANECDOTE—A Neat Education C D Of Truthful Events
87. ASIDE—A Speech Inaudible to Deaf Ears
88. ASSONANCE—A Similar Sound Of Non-consonants And Nouns to Create Effects
89. AUTOBIOGRAPHY—A Unique Telling Of Basic Incidents Of Glorified Reading And Personally Highlights You
90. BALLAD—Beautiful Artistic Language of Life And Death
91. BIOGRAPHY—Basic Incidents Of Glorified Reading And Publicly Highlights You
92. BLANK VERSE—Basic Language About New Knowledge Vacant End Rhyme Shows Expression
93. CHARACTER—Collection of Habits And Rituals Actors Clasp To Enrich Reality
94. CONNOTATIONS—Consists Of New Names Of The Added Terms In Our Numerous Suggestions
95. COUPLET—Consecutive Or Unified Poetry Lines Emphasizing Thoughts
96. DESCRIPTION—Details Emotional Senses Created or Re-created In Part To Inform Our Needs

97. DIALECT—Distinct Individually Accepted Language and Environmental Characteristic of Talking
98. DIALOGUE—Discussion Idles A Little Or Grows Urgent Eventually
99. DICTION—Decision In Choosing The Imagery Of Narratives
100. EPIC—Enormous Poem Indicating Courage
101. MOOD—Made Of Ornate Details

COOLPOSING LESSON PLANNING

The idea in school is to make teaching be the primary source of delivering curriculum and learning becomes the primary result of the curriculum. For this to happen, the two (teaching and learning) must merge as one. For this to happen, teaching may need to be rethought for certain purposes. While there is no such thing as one size fitting all, there is a sense of closeness to fit that can be modified for success. Unless the student truly knows a term, what it is, how it looks, what it does, why it does it, and when and where it does it, the learning of the term is rendered somewhat useless. The following is an example of a lesson plan that teaches one of the literary terms shown in a previous list.

Lesson teaching the literary term "Irony"

Objective:
Students will be able to learn and retain a literary term without the use of writing through identification of its purpose, definition, spelling, part of speech and parts of speech of its definition components, recognition of its meaning encased within its spelling, the "big picture" of its importance, and demonstrate their knowledge verbally when called on by the instructor.

Core Curriculum Content Standards:
3.a Speaking; 3.b Listening; and 3.c Viewing

Procedure:
1. *Students will be told a short poem that ends in irony *"As I was walking through the snow, I saw a bird that could not go, It could not fly or anything,*

Because it had a broken wing, So I lured it close with crumbs of bread, Then I took a rock and crushed its head!"

2. Students will be asked to explain the elements of the poem that created the irony (such as misdirection of the action; surprise ending)
3. Students will be told that the impact of the poem reflected the role of irony
4. Students will be shown the word "irony" on the board
5. Students will be told to view each letter as representative of a whole word
6. Students will be told the definition (It Reverses ON You)
7. Students will be asked to which part of speech "irony" belongs (noun)
8. Students will be asked to which parts of speech the entire definition belongs (It [pronoun]; Reverses [verb] ON [preposition] You [pronoun])
9. Students will physically move to posted signs around the room to show their knowledge of the parts of speech after hearing the questions (no talking)
10. Assessment can range from individual or team "races" to the posted signs to earn extra credit points as the activity reinforces the learning

Closure:

The literary term, "Irony" was learned through hearing a poem that showed how it was used, spelling, definition, recognition of part of speech in which it belongs, and parts of speech in which the components of its definition belongs, identification of mnemonic cues that help embed the meaning of the word within its spelling and increased retention of significant knowledge about the word through unifying relationships.

Homework:

Write a one-page response to this question: "How was today's lesson without writing different from the lessons that required writing? Did it allow you to feel anything new or "ironic"? Explain your answer using at least three examples" *Possible responses may include ease of remembering through sight and sound over writing; moving around to show knowledge instead of sitting; the large amount of learning that occurred from one five-letter *word; writing is not the only way one can learn; there was fun and laughter involved in learning; and the memory of the lesson will improve because there are more things to recall-running around, teamwork, challenge of winning, risk reduction through collaboration, and understanding a fairly difficult term in a manageable way].*

Coolposing Methods for Teaching Content

HUMANS ARE IDEALLY SET UP TO UNDERSTAND STORIES; NOT LOGIC. LOGIC DOES NOT IMPRINT AS DEEPLY AS STORIES DO.
[Stories capture elements that formal decision methods leave out. Logic tries to generalize, to strip the decision making from the specific context, to remove it from subjective emotions. Stories capture the context, capture the emotions . . . Stories are important cognitive events, for they encapsulate; into one compact package, information, knowledge, context, and emotion.] Which 13 original colonies group can you best recall?
Delaware (1787), Pennsylvania (1787), New Jersey (1787), Georgia (1788), Connecticut (1788), Massachusetts (1788), Maryland (1788), South Carolina (1788), New Hampshire (1788), Virginia (1788), New York (1788), North Carolina (1789) and Rhode Island (1790).

The Story of the 13 States that Ratified the Constitution:
Dela needed something to **Ware**, so she went to **Pennsylvania** to buy a **New Jersey**. She and, **Georgia**, **Connected** with a **Mass** of shoppers going to the **Mary Land** mall, on *Bargain Island*. They took the **South Car Line** and shared the **News** with **Hampshire** and **Virginia**, who just returned from **New York**. They then took the **North Car Line** and **Rhode** to the **Island**.

The Great Lakes *[largest group of fresh water lakes in the world]:*
Huron, Ontario, Michigan, Erie, Superior
Which lies entirely within the United States? (**Michigan**-it lies entirely within HOMES)
Which is the largest? (**Superior**-it means greatest)
Which is the third largest? (**Michigan**-it is the third letter in HOMES)
Which is the shallowest? (**Erie**-hallowest, as in Halloween, when things are eerie; least letters)
Which is the smallest? (**Ontario**-it ends with the last vowel of the group)

What spelling patterns are identified? (All start and end with either vowels or consonants)

PERSPECTIVES FOR TEACHING AMERICAN HISTORY:
Art Forms: Jazz (first), musical comedies, skyscrapers

Characteristic: "A Nation of Immigrants"

People: *Middle Atlantic States Region* [European, Black African, Latino, Asian], *Southern States Region* [early English, Irish, Scottish, Black Africans], *Midwestern Region* [Germany, Great Britain, Norway, Sweden, eastern and southern Europe], *Rocky Mountain States Region* [European, Black Africans, Mexican Americans, Native Americans, *Southwestern States region* [European, Black Africans, Mexican American, Native American], and *Pacific Coast States Region* [European, Black Africans, Mexican American, Asian and Native Americans]

---

* The first people to live in what is now the United States were "Indians" (Native Americans), Eskimos, and Hawaiians. The Indians and Eskimos are descended from peoples who migrated to North America from Asia thousands of years ago. The ancestors of the Hawaiians were Polynesians who sailed to what is now Hawaii from other Pacific islands about 2,000 years ago. Most white Americans trace their ancestry to Europe. The white population of the United States also includes Spanish-speaking people. Most Americans of Asian descent trace their ancestry to China, Indochina, Japan, or the Philippines. Many Americans take special pride in their origins. Most Black Americans are descendents of Africans brought to the United States as slaves during the 1600's, 1700's and 1800's and forced to work on plantations.

9

WHEN, WHERE, HOW, AND WHY BLACK MALES CRY

The measure of a man is his mouth

—Traditional

Interviews with Black male businessmen remain the best method to demystify the cultural context within which they learn and act out masculinity, male roles and values. It is also the ideal method to discover how they define anger, performance, impression management, social competence, pride, control, respect, and status. This chapter focuses on the actual voices of Black male businessmen as they describe their perceptions of their experiences of leading their businesses through interviews and transcripts.

The collective responses of these Black male businessmen will provide an overview of the common elements in experiencing leadership, how and why leadership is valuable, common elements of emotion felt as leaders, and significant influences regarding decision making and leadership styles. Black males cry artistically, at all times, and in full view of the world because it "be's" that way.

MUSIC PROMOTER

Arnold is a music promoter who has been in business for over 25 years. He owns a production company and is CEO of a cultural resource institute. He is very clear about his achievements and he motivates younger businessmen. His education has been the driving force behind his ability to inspire others and generate interest in large and successful musical events. He has a five-year plan that will place his company in a financially secure position and provide the community with high-level entertainment. He has a current need for financial assistance however he has operated within his budget thus far and appears capable of managing successfully in the future.

I = Interviewer
A = Arnold

I: I would like you to, as fully as you can, describe your experience of leading your business as a Black male businessman. You can take a couple of minutes to get into the experience. Include all that you feel is necessary. Start when you're ready.

A: Well, first, knowing my history and culture has been significant to me in leading people. Especially, in the kind of [jazz music promotion] business I have. Knowledge of God and awareness of my African heritage has helped me manage tough situations when I felt myself losing control. Knowing that Black people were the first to do business, based on the Bible, scholarly documentation and history of inventions and Blacks' relationships to them, helps. Spirituality has been key in my motivation to achieve success in business. I live, read and implement the strategies I learned about leadership when I took business courses in college. I never regretted it. I know my voice. It took a while, but I found it, and I know it.

I: You know your voice? Can you explain that?

A: There is little remaining to be invented or learned; all we have to do is add our voices to the body of creation. The trouble is you can't add your voice if you don't know it. I know mine, and I found it by listening to jazz. By listening . . . Not just listening to enjoy . . . listening to study. You see jazz is the significant vehicle for the transformation of society since it transports the genes of creation within its notes.

I: Is that the mission statement of your business?

A: Sort of . . . being an advocate for my passion *jazz+, which is the product I promote. My Black maleness requires me to lead in a righteous manner as a living memorial to my creator. Black businessmen must be able to walk among their people as leading figures in the family. They should have the respectable fear of their peers and colleagues.

I: How has your experience allowed you to gain the respectable fear of your peers?

A: By being aware of the way problems are avoided . . . problems are prevented by being detached from the troublemakers. That's the key to survival. That's how I do it. I overcome discrimination and other problems with slickness.

I: Slickness? Can you explain that?

A: Yes, you see when someone is harassing me, I can choose to get violent, ignorant or use some other aggressive behavior . . . but either way I lose. If I get arrested for hurting someone, even if I'm right, my business suffers. If I blow my cool, I lose my reputation and my ability to make a living. That's why I have to be slick. Slickness is being legitimate and hip at the same time. It's a way of being cool that requires skillful maneuvering to contribute to my business. You see, I deal with some of the slickest cats in the world; jazz musicians. Man, you haven't seen cool until you have to negotiate with some jazz bands for gigs.

I: What is that experience like?

A: Have you ever been "gritted on" (stared at) by a half dozen cats whose faces are so expressionless and cool that you don't know if they are mad or glad?

I: And you're not afraid?

A: I can't let them know it if I am. I have to keep my front up just like they keep theirs up. I have to stay in control of the situation. The tough guy look is part of their front to get me to either pay them more, let them play what they want, or some other benefit they can get. My business forces me to use my coolness and slickness to create the musical event through the promotion of the spectacle of uniqueness and flash. The icy cold stares from the musicians present a challenge for me to read. The good thing though, is their fans think they're cool, plus they can play. Hiring them is a necessary risk I have to keep taking. It's good for business. Deep, ain't it?

EDUCATIONAL CONSULTANT

Fred is an Educational Consultant with over 35 years experience as an educator. He is innovative, resourceful, and well respected. He is highly regarded as one of the foremost teacher trainers in the northeast. He envisions a future of educational change and he advises leaders on the post-modern strategies necessary for managers and leaders in education to stay productive and profitable.

I = Interviewer
F = Fred

I: I would like you to, as fully as you can, describe your experience of leading your business as a Black male businessman. You can take a couple of minutes to get into the experience. Include all that you feel is necessary. Start when you're ready.

F: Leading my [education consultant] business allows me to constantly relive my experience with education, which encouraged me to be as innovative in education as in any other field. I had no Black teachers until I went to college. Can you believe it? I saw my first Black teachers, and they were professors, when I was a college student. Those professors were sharp. I mean all of them. One was a tutor of King Haile Salaisee. Another professor was a philologist-one of only four in the world. I was fortunate to have had so many highly gifted teachers, and Black.

I: How did these teachers influence you; what were you able to take from each of them?

F: I used some of the psychology of all of those teachers, like "Don't smile until Christmas". Most of the students I encountered in my business did not have fathers, so I became a father figure. I was looked upon as cool because of the way I dressed and I used the latest slang in the appropriate situations. I even made up a slang dictionary for the students. I worked with mostly White and some Latino students early in my career. Students respected me and they knew I had rules and they remained supportive even when I chastised them.

I: How do you assess your effectiveness with your students? What are the indicators?

F: Many came back to see me after graduation to thank me. I emphasized that school supplies were tools and I treated them as if they worked for me. This motivated and inspired students to succeed at work. I constantly pushed the idea of higher education. My aunt was a college professor at [prominent Black university] where she had many prominent colleagues whom I met. Can you imagine how fortunate I was to have someone like that in my life?

Many students were unaware of college or how to prepare for it. I invented lesson strategies that created new views of attending college.

I: What lasting benefit do you think the students received from you?

F: I transformed many students' patterns of thinking of their capabilities. Many teachers are unaware of their total influence. I worked in high schools and jr. high schools as adviser to mostly White students. I counseled and taught at some of the most elite schools of engineering and science. I was associated with educated people all of my life. I got my masters degree from a college that has since shut down because too many Blacks were passing.

I: Did you create anything that was special, that they will remember?

F: Education created a fear of testing in students, even when they were qualified. I combated this fear by setting up counseling offices that mandated pre-SAT testing in the 9th grade. This innovation provided earlier exposure to testing for students. My past dictated my future. What was wrong had to be made right, no matter what method I had to mask it under. My business requires me to be creative in the education profession with development of new wave counseling and advising programs that will motivate students to excel scholastically in private and public learning institutions. I experienced frustration and elation each time I saw a student succeed despite the parents being drunk, drugged or missing. I was aware of siblings taking the parent's role of raising children.

There was a time I attempted to cope by taking a drink after getting home. Now I take a nap, leave the problems at work and cool out. My good education at [historically Black university] helped develop my leadership style, but the most important element was having a mother and father at home, pushing me to go to college and be successful. My parents were instrumental in helping shape my mental strength, self-esteem, and self-efficacy my talking to me as an equal; not as a subordinate. My environment played a role in my development; however, my socialization aided in my ability to code-switch and adjust to various needs of the situation.

I learned to dress appropriately and control the impression of others. Family played a major role in forming values that remain today. Before making decisions, I talk to those who are either authorities on the topic or knowledgeable of many things. My decisions include all the players in the game. My leadership style evolved from my college training, watching my mentors, and emulating some of the gang leaders of my youth, who were some of the smartest people I knew then. Gang leaders delegated responsibility to others, such as the warlord, runner of the old heads, juniors, midgets, etc. My discipline came from the Catholic Priests where I attended school as a boy.

PHOTOGRAPHER

Erwin is a photographer with over 25 years experience. His photo studio is one of the better-known Black owned facilities in the city. He does a large volume of business with weddings, special events, and especially high school graduations and proms. He retired from teaching and maintained many of the professional relations and much of the business with his former faculty members. He envisions a future of diversification in the photography industry, where changes in the world will dictate changes in the way photographers depict the world.

I = Interviewer
E = Erwin

I: I would like you to, as fully as you can, describe your experience of leading your business as a Black male businessman. You can take a couple of minutes to get into the experience. Include all that you feel is necessary. Start when you're ready.

E: Ethnic humor was a key coping mechanism that combined with creative speech and put customers effectively at ease. There was always a struggle because loans were difficult to get. I realized early that "brothers" got messed over by the banks. The value of pride rendering self-expression [in his photography business] provided the feeling of control to make shot selections, poses, scenery, and monetary considerations. Making decisions without having to check with anybody was like money.

Elements of emotion experienced were satisfaction, love of profession, and joy of accomplishing the goal of leading a thriving business. Skills that have helped in leadership are fronts, streetwise maneuvers and ability to not let things bother me, prayer, and belief in God. During decisions, I consider the benefit of the success then step out on faith. I mask my fear while negotiating with necessary fronts that provide balance. I was always a hustler and I used coping mechanisms to mask my fear of the uncertainty of business. I relied on self-esteem to manipulate clients that tended to complain.

I couldn't give money back, like larger businesses. I'd go broke. I had to lie. Customers often view White males as smarter or better and workers tend to not give as much effort to me as they would to White males. I know unskilled Whites. I became more thrift-conscious as a businessman since I knew all of the money was not mine. I learned to pay myself first. I don't need a bank loan now. My son learned business ethics and many of my former students that worked for me gained experience as apprentices and trainees under my leadership. I am a borderline diabetic with high blood pressure yet maintained a balanced diet to offset any major health-related issues.

CULTURAL ARTIST

Richard is a cultural artist who has a good reputation as a businessman and a fine artist. His clients are numerous and his artwork is costly, and appreciated. He is a well-dressed celebrity in the city who creates events that are talked about by the true art aficionados long after they end. The future is seen exciting with various styles of art blending to create new movements that will attract a new generation of art lovers.

I: Interviewer
R: Richard

I: I would like you to, as fully as you can, describe your experience of leading your business as a Black male businessman. You can take a couple of minutes to get into the experience. Include all that you feel is necessary. Start when you're ready.

R: Regarding Self in relation to loneliness, I relish peace witnessed by visiting my inner self by focusing inward for spiritual energy. Within me is God, somewhere, and divine intervention and spiritual intervention are keys in driving my success. People do not know the real me however; inward visits represent necessary chances to get invigorated in order to function at my physical peak. I resist distraction that would be costly to my [cultural artist] business. Retreating to my inner-self provides necessary loneliness that allows me to stay on my message, remain spontaneous, and open to any nuance of signals or messages attempting to reach me.

I need loneliness, which allows me to see things in a visceral manner. The solace of inner sanctum provides a setting for me to think of curves and flow and interconnectedness. During those moments when I explore solitude, I am aware of the intrigue of overlapping images and open to let things happen. I am able to approach business with a sense of confidence because I am not stressed out. The act of being alone is a coping mechanism used skillfully to provide time management, decision-making, holistic assessment, and unique blending of arts and sciences.

For me, Self in relation to excellence through self-achievement is one of my greatest concerns. It involves demanding most from me at all times. As a cultural artist in a burgeoning metropolis in northeastern United States, I seek competition because I am unchallenged in what I do. I have entered prisons without fear to teach my art because I knew my integrity was beyond formula. Excellence is my business goal and I am equally attentive to my unique wardrobe, which increases my confidence.

I am aware that my presence represents my product and clothing is key in establishing image. Every garment I purchase is the best available and my wardrobe is based on everything that works. In producing works of art, I am self-evaluative and willing to be patient and persistent in pursuit of excellence through the art medium. I achieve my desired result by doing one thing at a time before moving on. My work habits portray a sense of responsibility that sought to do things well first to avoid having to do them over. My leadership style is a synonym of Self in relation to creation.

Internal construction is the most important part of creation and demonstrated in my respect of spirituality. Through innovation, I do art because I love it. My love manifests through spiritual openness, which allows me to construct images without fear as if God has guided me. I am often inside of myself, leaving the world out, as I construct everything in preparation to completion time. I am driven by the idea that the mask never changes for a Black man or changes significantly for Blacks. I construct an intended image of cultural broker, which connects my experience as a presenter and performer of my art.

CLOTHING RETAILER

Charles is a clothing retailer with 33 years of business experience. He grew up in a business family and ownership was the focus of his existence. He has a fine reputation of fairness and he employs youth from the community. He has been located in a well-organized and successful business enclave that serves Black customers. He is politically conscious and he will not tolerate racial inequities. He is a role model to many young men in his community who do not have fathers.

I = Interviewer
C = Charles

I: I would like you to, as fully as you can, describe your experience of leading your business as a Black male businessman. You can take a couple of minutes to get into the experience. Include all that you feel is necessary. Start when you're ready.

C: My experience of owning and operating a business in Philadelphia was hard. Wanting badly to succeed yet enduring the daily uncertainty of commerce, with its high failure rate among Blacks is a constant struggle. I was prepared for mistakes by my mother, but I just was not ready for the frequency of the errors. I knew my Blackness created perceived problems but I decided early in life that I would be a model for others. I admitted that I felt Whites in business looked at me as an already read text when I entered various business environments seeking trade.

My retail clothing business has proved gratifying even though I am constantly operating as a risk-taker. Knowing there are no guarantees in business, my confidence comes from past victories. I had on-the-job training, better known in the business world as OJT. My mother owned a successful business and I watched her make it work with little education and formal training. When I was 10 or 12, I'm not sure which; I started to help around the [seamstress] shop. I soon learned how to operate the sewing machine, and soon I was on my way.

I had worked continually since I was a pre-teen. I recall working throughout my entire high school career. I understood all about the leap of faith businessmen talk so much about. I worked part-time, weekends and after school, occasionally taking time off to play football for my high school. I always had faith in myself. I guess it came from my family, who showed me that I could make a living without working for others. I refused to see someone take home the biggest check after I had worked just as hard or harder.

My mother was my role model. She was a female, single head of the house and she was as hardworking as anybody I knew. I used my own money to pay for all of my major expenses from high school including the prom, class trip, class ring and graduation. My mother taught me to be self-contained-anything I need, I must get it. I have been on my quest to succeed in business for over three decades. I have successfully owned and operated my business in a well-managed shopping enclave for 33 years. I left the city after high school to experience business practices in several other places. I returned to join the family enterprise after honing my merchandising skills at a department store.

The leadership experience had value for me all of the time. I cannot distinguish between myself and my business because the two are inseparable. The feeling became constant once I became a business owner-there was no quitting time. There are times when situations occur that may cause my perspective on things to change, but the feeling of leadership remains constant. The key emotion I feel is pleasure and satisfaction from having the ability to achieve my hopes and dreams as a business owner.

Owning a business provides me with stability in my life. High school contributed to my leadership ability because of the sports, work program, training for social skills by [principal F], the social setting of a co-ed education and my acquired social competence. I credit my early exposure to the social aspects of business through personal contact and my skill as a self-directed learner as keys to my business success. Internal motivation results from my inner-strength, which allowed me to survive two generations of customers patronizing my business.

I make decisions by studying the situation, doing my homework, and fact-finding. Once I get enough information, I make an educated decision that I will stand behind. Occasionally I take a calculated risk. I may take a chance but I do not gamble when making decisions about my business. I feel the business is an extension of me and represents my personality, socialization, genetics, friends and environment. I developed my style of leadership primarily from self-expression.

I recall those connected with my leadership experience as a teacher from high school that wrote daily philosophical phrases on the board, providing a strong male image for me to model. I also acknowledge my brother who worked at an automobile plant and a friend in a graduate program as closely connected with my experience. The behavioral changes I experienced were sacrifices by me and loved ones. I accept that there will be bad times.

Business is a relationship that requires total commitment. Without commitment, there are no successful moments. The changes that occur in business require selflessness of the career businessperson. I view my time in business as affecting others in life through neglectfulness in pursuit of success. My family suffered due to less time spent with my son, who later reaped benefits of profits from my business success. My significant other was neglected and later received benefit of later profits from business success. The inability to separate business from life issues may be detrimental to my health. I do not allow business to any longer consume me.

This concludes the section of the transcripts of interviews with the Black male businessmen, and their words combine to communicate the elements of *Coolposing* critical to providing balance and harmony to their lives as leaders. Their collective philosophy is the nine kinds of cool that is the essence of African culture: mysticism, accord, flexibility, vigor, change agency, collectivism, communicative individuality, verboseness, and shared-time perspective.

10

WHY BLACK MALES' STYLE CANNOT BE COPIED

A man's mind is his castle

—Richard Majors, PhD

The experience of leading a business as a Black male businessman is a constant struggle against racism, the imbalance of Blacks in powerful business positions, rage, disrespect, lack of financial support, loneliness, uncertainty, and overcoming tenseness by constructing fronts. Everything else related to the experience of leadership fades in comparison. The feeling of satisfaction, confidence, excellence, stability, and achievement grows from initially conquering the negative obstacles.

Feelings of value and worth spring forward in coping mechanisms. One of the measurements of success for Black male businessmen is the development of unique decision-making and leadership styles that do not reflect traditional values of the White male majority, nor reinforce White males' higher status. As the demands of business require change and innovation, Black male leaders maximize their time and product, consider their clients, mask their fear while negotiating, and consider the benefit of their decision before stepping out on faith.

Communalism is evident in many leadership styles as some Black males consult with their elders, experienced others, such as their parents, and trusted people before making decisions. Since success depends on each choice, some Black males anchor much of their faith in God, who they feel has made all things possible. Prayer, belief in God, trust in Devine guidance, and belief in the spirits of ancestors, influence some Black males in their leadership.

Despite faith, struggle remains a constant that is prepared for, anticipated, and even expected. Psychological defenses such as cool posing behaviors in the form of demeanor, speech, gestures, clothing and hairstyles, balance discomfort and provide self-esteem, control, and protection.

Drives for recognition, respect, success, unrestricted profit, emotional satisfaction, and control in making decisions, reduce anxiety, fear and doubt. Despite misclassification, Black male businessmen enjoy representing positive aspects of their communities. Being leading figures in their families and communities provides much of the motivation for some Black male businessmen to speak for improvements in business, and to pave the way for a better future for others.

Few Black males use negative autocratic, bureaucratic, or laissez-faire leadership characteristics. Democratic leadership, with the uniqueness of self-expression influences is most often used. Because of the long work hours, many Black males neglect family members to make their businesses successful.

Sacrifices experienced in leading businesses take an enormous toll on Black males however, through survival mechanisms such as shucking, ethnic humor, and inversion; they provide balance. The need to make neighborhood friends, family, wives, mentors, and extended family members proud is a strong influence for Black males to withstand hardship and endure. They continue despite customers' often viewing White males as higher status, and some workers not giving as much effort as they give for White males.

Changes from their leadership experience include increased thrift consciousness, newly acquired expertise, more realistic world-views, hardening of their style for protection, flexibility, restructuring of their minds, patience, confidence, self-reliance, and invention. The integration of newly learned strategies is the prime element of successful businessmen.

Critical thinking skills and mind games usually developed early in the businessmen socialization are sources of leadership styles. Loners are frequently the most resilient to setbacks because of their high proficiency in internal construction enabling them to imagine themselves out of dilemmas. Many Black male businessmen covet being clever or slick.

The historically short life expectancy of Black males in America is a concern of all businessmen. Some are borderline diabetics with high blood pressure who maintained balanced diets to prevent health issues. Attempts at no distraction by institutional racism in business help some Black males show no excessive stress. Some have vowed to remain tough and detached as a survival mechanism and stress reducing strategy. Coping skills offset physical problems by reducing stress and maintaining equilibrium.

Several businessmen that survived hernia operations enjoy a stress-free demeanor. Overall, attempts to feel invigorated by exercise to maintain good physical health helps assure others of increased longevity, and to prove "we are not our past".

The experience of leadership and its influences for Black male businessmen is primarily an affective functioning or spiritual concern. The ability to construct adequate coping mechanisms to provide strength and pride through the crisis of business operation plays an important part in reaching desired levels of success. Leadership experience forces Black males to willingly face an outside crisis of negative notions by others, and come out of the crisis, unmarked.

Those who are most in touch with their emotions during the crisis of business leadership, rather than denying or minimizing their feelings, are those who survive the crisis best and are most successful. These businessmen do not represent the most technically skilled, but the coolest and most poised leaders, and tend to be the most prepared to be effective during future crises. The leadership experience is the pursuit of the rewards of ownership: freedom, empowerment and voice. These rewards are frequently unattainable and made near impossible by societal obstacles.

Leadership forces extreme sacrifice and one reaches out further to fulfill the hope than few things imaginable. In the reaching, frustration, doubt and rage is experienced, yet is countered by the urge to make others proud, share good fortune with family, and make up for the neglect of significant others for business success. Yearning for fulfillment is motivation equally by past influences, such as ancestors, as well as by future concerns of individual sense of achievement.

Leadership experience is the urge for public recognition, to inspire and motivate others, to offer employment opportunities, and gain celebrity status for some. Desperation and triumph live together in the leadership experience as one builds the bridge as it is crossed. Fear is masked and established performances cover their doubt as the level of discomfort increases to affect the achievement in a positive direction. Leaders speak the language of values, and when none exists, they create one through verboseness that connects their followers with the rest of the world. Influences of leaders are deeply rooted, which allows the servant-like leader to view any problem as inside him, and not outside. In this way, the change process starts in the leader, and not outside, in society.

Leadership experience is an original approach by Black males to discover how to make power work *for* them, since they have centuries of knowledge of the way power works *on* them. Personal time, and not clock time is the tool that most reflects the Black male leader. Time is precious; time is money.

The scarcity of time enhances its value and forces Black males to increase its value by creating a non-standard time-"Colored People's (CP) Time"-that is not restricted by the clock. "CP Time" rejects the linear view of time and replaces it with a far richer complex idea of working time. The best time for the Black male occurs after hours, around midnight, in the wee small hours of the morning, or when the nighttime is the right time.

The thought regarding "CP Time" is that White males control the day, and Black males *own* the night.

Leadership experience and its influences of Black male businessmen reflect seeing in a new way. The influence of viewing from a deeply feeling, slightly irrational and emotional perspective, cause some Black males to dedicate themselves to transforming their business to a healing practice or else prepare for society's destruction. Led by the intervention of the highest power to conduct business righteously creates the urge to connect holistically to the task of leading. Success is not measurable and the integrity realized as a leader is valued by a sense of unchallenged expertise and fearlessness in decision-making. The awareness by Black male businessmen that they represent their products is the basic energy to initiate and sustain action to translate intentions into reality. Some Black males, like great men before them who determined the course of history, influence movements and prevent others from leading their organizations in another, unwanted direction.

Leading is experienced through the impact on the Self far more frequently than on others. The influences of self-help establish beliefs that show through leaders' intentions. The behavior of leaders attempts to close the gap of who they are and who they hope or imagine themselves to be. Invention provides self-esteem and stimulates established performances that increase competence.

The role as leader stops any sense of inferiority and fuels further construction of uniqueness. The knowledge of history, culture, heritage, and Allah/God inspires and motivates. Spirituality reinforces itself through reflections of troubled business experiences from which businessmen seek rescue, such as attempts at hostile takeovers and much needed financial support. Eternal gratefulness goes to Allah/God, who is love and has lifted many.

The leadership experience and its influence on Black male business is less of a mystery than contradiction. The elusiveness of control that is felt in making choices that matter is positive and negative. It is Positive in its value, satisfaction, and fulfillment of one's love of his profession, yet it is negative in its loneliness, competition, obstacles, and the rarity of Black males enjoying success. Like the mysterious powers possessed by the shaman, Black male businessmen *read* people, use spiritual skill to work through painful injuries, grow from failures, thrive on anxiety, and envision victory while encircled by an army of their enemies. Their

Coping mechanism in the form of coolness, masks their fear, and provide strength and pride.

Finally, the leadership experience and its influence on Black male businessmen reflect inward in silence. Their emotions remain in check beneath the visible surface as their critical thinking skills continue to solve problems that are threatening the future of their enterprises. Their self-imposed restraint is preferred to externally imposed restrictions. Cool outward appearances guard the secret of the inner fires that are aflame and fueled by responsibility, mission, commitment, and honor in serving at the leadership level. Inversion provides the appropriate misdirection, which further enables their undetected passions to burn, and produces a brighter burning flame of leadership. The flames symbolize the idea that the closer one comes to danger more brightly do the ways into salvation and redemption glow. Through glowing spirits, and scorched and charred memories of a guarded, fragile past, when discovery meant defeat or even death, Black males secretly signal each other that where the danger exists, *Coolposing* provides the saving power.

THE END

Index

The next section spotlights specific inventions and data on Black male inventors.

COMMUNICATIONS INVENTIONS

The following list of inventions by Black male businessmen is a partial display of the inventiveness of this group in communications. Note that he dates on many of the inventions are in the 1800s, which in some cases is a time that is less than a full generation after the abolishment of slavery. The variety of inventions and their usefulness is a testament to the resourcefulness of a group that has existed in the margin of society, yet summoned the strength to perform on the main stage:

1. Telephone System and Apparatus: Granville T. Woods, Cincinnati, Ohio, October 11, 1887, Patent Number: 371,241-Woods' invention improved transmission of voice and sound over telephone, making it easier to hear and understand. It also reduced interference from neighboring lines.
2. Letter Box: Philip B. Downing, Boston, Massachusetts, October 27, 1891, Patent Number: 462,093-Downing designed mailbox to help protect mail and make it easily accessible by mail carrier.
3. Type Writing Machine: Lee S. Burridge and Newman R. Marshman, New York, New York, April 7, 1885, Patent Number: 315,366-Burridge and Marshman improved appearance of letters and documents, making them easier to read.
4. Fountain Pen: William B. Purvis, Philadelphia, Pennsylvania, January 7, 1890, Patent Number: 419,065-Purvis' first pocket fountain pen made writing less cumbersome because it eliminated need for carrying separate bottle of ink, known as an *ink well*. The new invention had built-in ink reservoir that would automatically feed ink to pen.
5. Player Piano: Joseph H. Dickinson, Cranford, New Jersey, June 11, 1912, Patent Number: 1,028,996-Dickinson's invention was used to play for all occasions and had repertoire from dance to sing-a-long tunes.

---

6. Railway Telegraphy: Granville T. Woods, Cincinnati, Ohio, August 28, 1888, Patent Number: 388,803-Woods' invention led to major improvements in railway communication by improving safety and reducing operating cost for railway company.

7. Electric Lamp: Lewis H. Latimer and Joseph V. Nichols, New York, New York, September 13, 1881, Patent Number: 247,097-Latimer and Nichols simplified construction of electric lamp, which made it more durable and effective. It also reduced price of electric lamp. In addition, by enclosing wires or filaments, in pear-shaped transparent receiver, these men invented light bulb-which Thomas Edison is credited with as principal inventor of Edison Pioneers project.

8. Guitar: Robert F. Flemmings, Jr., Melrose, Massachusetts, March 30, 1886, Patent Number: 338,727-Because of improvements by Flemmings, musicians experienced improved melodic tones and increased volume in this string instrument. Flemmings also made guitar more sensitive to touch, which made it easier on fingers while playing.

9. Printing Press: W. A. Lavalette, Washington, D.C., September 17, 1878, Patent Number: 208,184-Lavalette made overall improvements to earlier model, which made it faster, easier to use and actual print easier to read.

10. Arm for Recording Machine: Joseph Hunter Dickinson, Cranford, New Jersey, January 8, 1918, Patent Number: 1,252,411-Dickinson's invention helped to improve sound quality of earlier model of record player. The tone arm gave richer tone to record and horn helped to control volume so that music can be heard from greater distance.

11. Relay-Instrument: Granville T. Woods, Cincinnati, Ohio, June 7, 1887, Patent Number: 364,619-Woods' invention was similar to modern telephone, and used combinations of electricity and magnets, or an automatic electromagnetic device, that responded to small current or voltage change by activating switches or other devices in an electric circuit. This improved construction and sensitivity of inductive telegraphy (Cord, 2003).

FOOD INVENTIONS

The following list of inventions by Black male businessmans is a partial display of the inventiveness of this group in food service, preparation, storage and related issues. What is to be noted is the usefulness of these items today as well as at the time of their invention. With very little formal education or professional-style training, thes Black males utilized the mysticism inherent in *EntrepreCool*, to produce a result much more complete than the available resources foresaw:

1. Refrigerator: John Stanard, Newark, New Jersey, July 14, 1891, Patent Number: 455,891-Stanard improved on original icebox by putting cold-air ducts or holes in special areas to help air circulate within refrigerator in order to keep foods fresher. He also provided a special place to keep drinking water separate from food to help keep it cool and not pick up smells and flavors of foods inside.
2. Corn Silker: R. P. Scott, August 7, 1894, Patent Number: 524,223-Scott's invention quickly and efficiently removed outer green husks and silk-like fibers on inside, called corn silk, which are difficult and time consuming to discard.
3. Potato Digger: F. J. Wood, April 23, 1895, Patent Number: 537,953-Wood's invention made harvesting potatoes for farmer lot faster and easier. The potato digger dug into ground to loosen dirt, making it easier for pickers to scoop potatoes from ground.
4. Lemon Squeezer: J. T. White, December 8, 1896, Patent Number: 572,849-White's invention was first juicer and made it easier to squeeze all of juice out of lemon without getting seeds and lot of pulp; it was also neater because it prevented juice from squirting all over.
5. Ice Cream Mold and Disher: Alfred L. Cralle, Pittsburgh, Pennsylvania, February 2, 1897, Patent Number: 576,395-Cralle's invention allowed one-hand operation for perfectly round portions of ice cream to fit neatly onto cones or plates.
6. Kneading Machine: Joseph Lee, Auburndale, Massachusetts, August 7, 1894, Patent Number: 524,042-Lee's invention would mix and knead dough by eliminating for cook pushing back and forth, pounding and shaping to make baking more enjoyable.

7. Churn: Albert C. Richardson, South Frankfort, Michigan, February 17, 1891, Patent Number: 446,470-Richardson improved churn by putting glass on two sides of churn so that it would be easier to tell when butter was ready without opening churn. In addition, he made it easier to remove butter by placing plate inside churn for butter to be placed.
8. Improvement in Sugar Making: Norbert Rillieux, New Orleans, Louisiana, December 10, 1846, Patent Number: 4879-Rillieux invented new and improved method of making sugar, which involved heating, evaporating and cooling of liquids especially intended for manufacture of sugar.
9. Biscuit Cutter: Alexander P. Ashbourne, Oakland, California, November 30, 1875, Patent Number: 170,460-Ashbourne's invention was an improvement that helped to cut creative shapes into lots of biscuits, cakes or cookies at once.
10. Steam Table: George W. Kelley, Norfolk, Virginia, October 26, 1897, Patent Number: 592,591-Kelley made improvements on portable steam table-one that moves around from table to table in restaurant-by providing different compartments for many types of food and drinks at once (Cord, 2003).

WESTERN EXPANSION AND SETTLEMENT INVENTIONS

The following list of inventions by Black male businessmans is to show a partial display of the inventiveness exhibited by this group in technology and industry. Of special note in this section is the idea that a people primarily viewed as field hands and planters contributed to a movement that required daring, vision and engineering skills. The accumulative affect of the innovation in this section should silence the critics who have claimed that the African was primarily a beast of burden:

1. Running Gear: John W. West, Saylorville, Iowa, October 8, 1870, Patent Number: 108,419-West's invention was a major improvement in wagons. By making hind wheels larger than front wheels and hind axle higher than front axle, West helped to distribute the weight of load in such a way to help propel and

push the load forward. This provided less strain on horse and made traveling a lot faster.

2. Smoke Stacks for Locomotives: Landrow Bell, Washington, D.C., May 23, 1871, Patent Number: 115,153-Bell's invention helped to arrest flying sparks and cinders, making train travel much safer.

3. Shampoo Head Rest: C. O. Bailiff, Kalamazoo, Michigan, October 11, 1898, Patent Number: 612,008-Bailiff's invention made shampooing more comfortable because it attached to back of chair giving support to head so person was able to lean backward for water to run down hair instead of face.

4. Bridle Bit: Lincoln F. Brown, Xenia, Ohio, October 25, 1892, Patent Number: 484,994-Brown invented an improvement to help control a runaway horse.

5. Riding Saddle: William D. Davis, Fort Assinniboine, Montana, October 6, 1896, Patent Number: 568,939-Davis' riding saddle was invented to help make horseback riding more comfortable and safer. He improved saddle by making it easier to give adjustment, strength and elasticity to seat of saddle. Davis further improved saddle by increasing durability of stirrup saddle strings and straps.

6. Bag Closure: A. L. Ross, New York, New York, June 7, 1898, Patent Number: 605,343-Ross' invention assisted pioneers, who traveled west to settle new land with a trash bag that was used for storing ashes, paper, bottles and other necessities. When bag was full, it was taken off a hook and its mouth closed while locking frame hinges together so that bag can be moved without losing its contents.

7. Shoe Lasting Machine: Jan E. Matzelinger, March 20, 1883, Patent Number: 272,207-Matzelinger's invention helped shoe cobbler work faster sewing tops of shoes and boots to soles. This also produced shoes that were made better and lasted longer.

8. Overboot for Horses: Robert Coates, Washington, D.C., April 19, 1892, Patent Number-Coate's invention prevented horse from slipping and sliding when overboot was used during sleety and rainy weather.

9. Horseshoe: Oscar E. Brown, Buffalo, New York, August 23, 1892, Patent Number: 481,271-Brown made horseshoe more comfortable and easier to fit on horse by inventing a way to cushion horseshoe so that it would relieve pressure from horse and make taking care of horseshoe easier for Blacksmith (Cord, 2003).

TELEVISION PRODUCER

Bill is a television producer with experience in the commercial, industrial and public sectors. He owns a production company that records audio and visual music performances. His education, both in the schools and in the risky business of freelance production has been his strongest influence to leadership of his business. He makes developing youth a key principle of his business. He provides exposure to rising artists by giving them a quality audio-visual presentation, however he works with them to keep the cost down.

I = Interviewer
B = Bill

I: How do you as a Black male businessman perceive and describe your experience of leading your business?

B: There has always been a struggle against racism in the film media, which has taken many good, strong producers down. My faith has been challenged continually as I had to overcome the exhaustion resulting from the negative experiences, and I am sure it has affected my career. I had to deal with the hardship of being at peace with the significant imbalance of people of color in decision-making roles in the media. I was dedicated, through my faith and belief in God to make an impact in the all-important business of opinion shaping and image making.

I: Describe a time when leadership experience had particular value to you.

B: There seems to be a constant time when I feel valued and thankful that I had a chance to call the shots and make the final cut in the production studio, because the real ideas are made at the final cut. My role provides a sense of accomplishment for me and I feel doubly pleased when many see a successful production and I am called upon to take a bow. I believe we as a people have made much progress in getting Blacks trained in TV production and employment in the media.

I: If leadership helped you feel emotion, please describe what this has been like for you. Share all thoughts, perceptions and feelings of emotion you can recall until you have no more to say.

B: Frustration has been the longest lasting feeling that I recall. Frustration is often related to the enormous amounts of time required to produce a quality film. There are many things that test my faith and time is one. The long periods of waiting while everything is done well, and slow, gets to me at times. Anxiety and doubt seem to go hand in hand when filming is taking place. There is always the nervousness that things will go wrong. The success of the productions never fail to bring relief and pleasure. Joy is probably the best word that I sense when I feel everything has worked out fine.

I: Describe mental, physical, spiritual or other skills you have that that you believe were most helpful in your becoming a leader.

B: The idea of patience is the key skill to have in the production field, because good things take a long time to make happen. There has to be skills in thinking clearly and working well under pressure because time is never plentiful. There is always pressure to make the deadlines.

I: Describe your process of decision-making.

B: I am always concerned about the audience's needs. I believe looking out for the audience is the central focus of a good producer, because the audience controls the success or failure of the production. Decisions are made in regards to the larger demand, then the smaller demands require time. I enjoy addressing the lesser demands that also affect the rights of the underrepresented among us.

I: How did you develop your leadership style?

B: I was driven to overcome my dyslexia which produced a stronger determination within me than had I not had a disability. The challenge of the dyslexia kept me on my toes and concentrating harder than usual. I became intense, focused, and introverted. Introverted-ness helped me because it kept me inwardly focused and made it easier for ideas to develop within me.

FINANCIAL MANGER

Reggie is a financial manager who is aggressively building wealth through adventurous investments. He works with youth on the weekends, providing a strong role model, and teaches them how to handle money and make good decisions. The future is as a place that is created as opposed to a place that already exists. Financial matters are a means to a non-materialistic end. He spends a lot of time planning for new ways to educate youth.

I: Interviewer
R: Reggie

I: How do you, as a Black male businessman, perceive and describe your experience of leading your business?

R: I felt many anxious moments based on the risks and uncertainty of business. I remained focused in the midst of my crises by projecting a strong front. I made business deals with people I had to trust after a short relationship. This causes much uncertainty in me. I made myself comfortable with business associates by reflecting inward to my natural sense of reading people. I was discriminated against but refused to let it change my optimism. I made White business friends and trusted them. I shared business secrets with those who shared with me. Gaining recognition as a businessman pleased me a lot, especially when I was in the company of other business leaders. It gave the sense of value and worth and let others see me as a responsible person. The pressure placed on myself makes me perform better in other areas than business. Respect shown gives value to my life. Problems in the finance field are clearer since getting involved with business organizations that educate and train others based on their reputations as owners and community advocates. My feelings of anxiety, fear, doubt, and uncertainty are common. There are good moments where happiness is present but not long lasting, because the nature of business is highs and lows. The good feelings are remembered longer, though. My fear is covered by the front so I can mix into the mainstream of the business where a smile or a pleasant expression is wanted. I feel panic every week for one reason or another and I have to hide my fear, or else the customers or my competition will eat me up.

I laugh a lot because humor is needed, especially in the shaky financial field. I have to keep my spirits up with so much doubt around. I guess money and doubt goes together. Good math skills and spirited teachers set my foundation for business. I had some great people around me. I guess I was blessed with good analytical skills or something, because even though I am naturally curious, I never tried drugs and I never really liked drinking. When I was at parties, I even had friends who would try to get me to take a drink. I was too strong, and I refused and still had a good time. I was one of the smart students in school, so I never gave in when I knew something wasn't good for me. You know, I believe I had a highly developed problem-solving trait. Maybe it was God-given. I refused to give up when all angles seemed closed because it helped me create the desire to persist in the face of failure. My belief in my creator provides me with answers. Good physical condition has been an asset to get into work daily and complete all my tasks. My problems are broken down into percentages, such as a pie chart or something. The most essential portion of the problem is given a larger percentage of my time, and attacked first. Each segment of the problem is then approached in descending order, with the least significant approached last. All angles are considered when I solve problems. Growing up, my neighborhood friends were very clever and to stay up with them helped me think better. Good critical thinking skills were necessary to be able to hang with them. Mind games were a major part of growing up.

BOOKSELLER

Kevin is a bookseller and education consultant who has been ordained as a minister. He has an Ivy League education and a strong background in business management. He has a young family, which he spends a lot of time with, and very meticulously arranges his schedule between selling, consulting and preaching. His focus is on spirituality, which he uses as a guide for his life, and on which he bases his morals and ethics. His plans include pasturing a church.

I = Interviewer
K = Kevin

I: How do you, as a Black male businessman, perceive and describe your experience of leading your business?

K: Success leads to more opportunities. Loneliness is because of the rarity of Blacks in the bookselling business, which creates uniqueness.

I: Uniqueness?

K: Yes, uniqueness through individuality of Blackness. Remembered in a positive light uniqueness is experienced as rare moments of pleasure and innovation within overcoming obstacles.

I: How was leadership valuable for you?

K: I had an opportunity to lead a territory by example. This allowed me to experience success, which is the biggest challenge. I discovered that Self is the biggest competition. I know success pays the bills and creates profit. I bring value to customers by seeing the need and addressing it with expertise.

I: What are emotions you relate to your experience?

K: The joy of reaching the sales goals of the business and learning to live with the failures. Anxiety of the position is out-weighed by joy. The pleasure of helping others is a central goal. A sense of accomplishment is worth being in business of accomplishment to the instructional outcomes. Satisfaction is the number one feeling in the business field.

I: What influences your leadership style?

K: The ability to read people well is an asset in my business, which means having the ability to tell if others are serious about buying. This is a spiritual skill that I do not fully understand; it develops when God is placed higher in priority. The job is very physical and I have pushed on through injuries to be successful. When making decisions I look at enrollment to determine the number of books that can be sold. Larger volumes allow maximization of time and product. My leadership style was determined over a period as an outgrowth of my personality and values. Have positive selling style that showed value and places self in role of customer. My style is to be a consultant working with professors and students.

ATTORNEY

Warren is an attorney at law who was involved with leadership activities since a teen in college. He was mentored by a strong Black male attorney at law and was directed to fight for the civil rights of the disadvantaged. He has a strong spiritual foundation and is very active in church. His future involves expansion of his talents to the arts and entrainment field as agent, producer, manager, and legal representative.

I = Interviewer
W = Warren

I: How do you, as a Black male businessman, perceive and describe your experience of leading your business?

W: Overcoming oppression that was not witnessed by Whites is a major element of my experience. Working harder, longer and for less money than if I worked for others was hard to take at first. I accepted the risk of business. I experienced tenseness that I overcame with fronts. I witnessed satisfaction related to ownership. Law is all I know and it seems natural. I made decisions on the spot and felt confident with them. Each court appearance helped me grow and excel. Taking responsibility for all outcomes gave me satisfaction and joy. I was pleased with my ability to meet challenges. I covered the spectrum of feelings. I had high expectations, a good upbringing, a decent family, and great teachers in my environment. There was not much industry in the south so I was driven to be a professional. I guess there was a desire deep within me. I prepare as much as possible and pray. God's grace and mercy helps me. There is a genuine urge to make good for personal reasons. I want so badly to make my family proud. My role models were [great Black lawyer] and my father, who was a perfectionist. I had friends from the 60s civil rights movement. I guess I am meaner and more cynical than I used to be. The job has made me form hardness for protection. Many friends and even family members benefited from my free or discounted legal services. They all supported me through my career. I feel no extra stress. I have developed the ability to manage stress by not focusing on it. Stress does not distract me.

EDUCATION ADMINISTRATOR

Virgil is an education administrator who has managed various organizations in a creative manner. He prides himself on his ability to identify paradigm shifts and become an early innovator. His ideas have had positive influence in shaping the minds of many educators, administrators and learners. His future appears set on finding his ideas implemented throughout the country.

I = Interviewer
V = Virgil

I: How do you, as a Black male businessman, perceive and describe your experience of leading your business?

V: The experience has been steeped in uncertainty yet there was excitement connected to the idea of owning something. The responsibility of knowing there is no one to blame but myself for mistakes was an ongoing motivation to learn the inside of the business and continue to improve and update skills. I retained a sense of pride being in charge, not having to wait for orders. My experience gave me a chance to build upon personal experiences and develop a unique business full of innovations.

The chance to take the lead in decision-making was a rewarding benefit of ownership. I did not have to shape my business to please White men and White males were not given any higher status than anyone else. Ideas for the business were for the empowerment of the audience, both Black and White and they appreciated the company's product. I was fearful at times yet held myself together in a dignified manner in crisis. I gained respect in the industry and in my community as an businessman, despite not being rich.

As owner of a business I was interviewed by a radio station and I felt confidence and high self esteem as the guest of the show. The audience at home called in with questions, which gave me a great sense of achievement as an owner. I was heard by thousands of people who were interested in my story of leaving one industry as a success and gaining success in the new industry. As the leader of my business, I was given the responsibility of organizing presentations for large audiences. I had to create and innovate often.

My intuition or ability to imagine so clearly that I can nearly see the future is a skill that has helped me as leader. When choices have to be made quickly I rely on my intuition, which I believe links me spiritually to my creator who advises me. The good health that I have maintained is necessary for me to succeed daily in executing my duties. I imagine the results of the decision as early as possible. I look beyond the moment for clues of what to do.

I check past practices and consider the odds of success then I weigh the options. My laid back reserved approach was developed from a lifetime of observing successful people. The most prominent people in my memory were teachers. Several good friends have supported my efforts for decades. My family has been a strong support system. The biggest behavioral change that I recall was the confidence and self reliance of knowing that I can succeed under the most trying circumstances. I changed the way I greeted others, with more enthusiasm. I created the role of a winner. I became more successful. The main bodily change was a health-related issue that I overlooked because of the pace of the business.

FREE-LANCE REPORTER/PHOTOGRAPHER

Mango is a free-lance reporter and photographer working in the northeastern United States. He has worked for highly visible political figures and well known celebrities. He profited in business and is a strong supporter of Afro-centric expression.

He sees the future as one of challenge and scarcity of opportunities for Blacks and other minorities.

I = Interviewer
M = Mango

I: How do you, as a Black male businessman, perceive and describe your experience of leading your business?

M: The common elements in my experience of leadership is rage felt by many years related to disrespect and knowledge of how to disguise it. No one wants to be viewed as a "crybaby" in life, especially an adult, so I find ways of disguising my pain through laughter, comical behavior at times and sly remarks. This keeps the attention off of me. I think some people are on to me, but I won't even let them know they're on to me-I keep on fronting.

Leadership is valuable to me because it creates a way for me to speak out on my beliefs and those in my company. I can voice my opinion on beliefs, values and concerns of the community as a leader. When I fill the role I fill, I become bigger in every sense of the word. My role as leader makes movement possible by understanding media and having a degree of media savvy. I experienced emotion mainly inside. I am not a complainer, but I get disgusted easily, so I know disgust with racism is a big thing with me. I carry my disgust to the level of the city and state government.

I won't allow myself to get worried about Bush's war, so I maintain my faith that there will be a brighter day ahead; that is the title of one of the songs the choir sings in church. I believe in God, and will never deny it. It's a shame I can't say the same about everybody. Because of my belief, I can mask my fear with faith, and that gives me confidence when I'm in crowds. My feeling of what influenced me to become any kind of leader was knowledge of my past and the painfulness of the whole thing.

God truly had his eyes on the sparrow, and I still knew some kind of way he was watching me. Even when I think about the past atrocities of my people, I get stronger and not weaker. In fact, it allows me to get a better understanding of my mission and my true reason for wanting to lead. My faith in my almighty creator and respect for all those who came before me guide me through this world. Even today, one of the hardest things in the world is making a decision. I am sure that I can almost immediately feel the answer. What to they call that? Yeah, intuition, that's it.

I have intuition of right and wrong and that is what leads my choices. First, I have to know the facts, then my feelings take over. I don't just make a decision because it has to me made. I read about the situation, then I really look at the faces of the people who will be affected by my decision. There are actually signs in their faces telling me what to do. I still read about the issues, view the media, write or email, and speak about the topic to be decided on. My style came from the streets.

My environment growing up was rough but I was not seriously affected by it. I saw bad things happen and I saw people hurt, but I chose not to do it and that has made the difference. My spirit was not bad, I guess. I made friends with the African type groups and the people were all cool. I could talk with them and learn something every time. I grew up hearing jazz, cultural drumming, and soul music and I looked at African art a lot.

REFERENCES

Amen, R. (1990). *Metu neter vol. 1; The great oracle of tehuti and the Egyptian system of spiritual cultivation.* New York: Khamit Corp.

The Armstrong Association. (1918). *The Negro in business in philadelphia: An investigation by the association of business.* Philadelphia: The Armstrong Association Publishing Company.

Asante, M., & Mattson, M. (1992). *The historical and cultural atlas of black americans.* New York: Macmillan Publishing Company.

Asante, M., & Asante, K. (1990). *African culture: The rhythms of unity.* Trenton, NJ: Africa World Press, Inc.

Asante, M. (1988). *Afrocentricity.* Trenton, NJ: Africa World Press.

Banks, J. (2000). *Multicultural education, transformative knowledge, and action.* Seattle, WA: Teachers College Press.

Bass, B. (1990). *Bass & stogdill's handbook of leadership; Theory, research, and managerial applications* (3rd ed.). New York; The Free Press.

Batey, S. (1999). The humanities and social sciences. *Dissertation Abstracts International, 60, 4,* 1342A.

Begley, S. (2002, October 25). Eyewitnesses to crime are often blinded by shock, adrenaline. *The Wall Street Journal,* B1.

Bell, G. (2002). *In the black: A history of African Americans on wall street.* New York: John Wiley & Sons, Inc.

Bennett, L. (2001). *Before the mayflower: A history of black America* (7th Rev. ed.). New York: Penquin Books.

Berk, L. (1997). *Child development* (4th ed.). Boston: Allyn and Bacon.

Bertalanffy, L. (2001). *General system theory: Foundations, development, applications* (Rev. ed.). New York: George Braziller.

Blockson, C. (2001). *Pennsylvania's black history.* Philadelphia: Portfolio Associates.

Bogle, R. (2001). *Toms, coons, mulattos, bucks and pickininies.* New York: Penquin Books.

Bolster, W. (1998). *Black jacks: African American seamen in the age of sail.* London: Harvard University Press.

Booker, C. (2000). *I will wear no chain!: A social history of black males.* Westport, CT: Praeger.

Boyd, H., & Allen, R. (1995). *Brotherman: The odyssey of black men in americai.* New York: Ballantine Books.

Boykins, W. (1983). The academic performance of afro-american children. In *Achievement and achievement motives,* ed. J. Spence. SanFrancisco: W.H. Freeman.

Bradford, W. (2003, March). The wealth of businessmanship for black and white families in the u.s. *Review of Income& Wealth, 49,* 89-118.

Brown, D. (2002, November). African 161pasturing with advanced degrees turn to businessmanship. *Black Enterprise, 33,* 36.

Butler, J. (1995, Fall). Businessmanship and the advantages of the inner city: How to augment the porter thesis. *Review of Black Political Economy, 24,* 39-50.

Carter, N., Gartner, W., & Greene, P. (2002). The career reasons of minority nascent Businessmans. *Academy of Management Proceedings,* 1-6.

Clegg, S., Hardy, C., & Nord, W. (2001). *Handbook of organization studies.* London: Sage Publications.

Cohen, C., & Nee, E. (2000, April). Educational attainment and sex differentials in casturi casturin communities. *American Behavioral Scientist, 43,* 1159-1207.

Cooper, R., & Sawaf, A. (1997). *Executive eq: Emotional intelligence in leadership and organizations.* New York: The Berkley Publishing Group.

Cord, M. (2003). We did it; They hid it. *Black Inventions, 1,* 1-25.

Cose, E. (2002). *The envy of the world: On being black in America.* New York: Washington Square Press.

Courtland, L. (1991). Empowering young black males. *Information Analyses of University of Michigan, 73,* 1-5, retrieved on July 6, 2003 from http://ericfacility.net/ericdigests/ed341887.html

Creswell, J. (1994). *Research design: Qualitative & quantitative approaches.* London: Sage Publications.

Crockett, R. (2003) Memo to the supreme court: Diversity is good business. *BusinessWeek*, 96.

Cross, G. (2004). *Cool pose: A phenomenological study of leadership of black male entrepreneurs.* Published Doctoral Dissertation, University of Phoenix, Phoenix, Arizona.

Cummings, S. (1999). African American entrepreneurship in the suburbs: Protected markets and enclave business development, *Journal of the American Planning, 65,* 3-20.

Drs. Davis, S., Jenkins, G. & Hunt, R. (2002). *The pact: Three young men make a promise and fulfill a dream.* New York: Riverhead Books.

DuBois, W.E.B. (1899/1973). *The philadelphia negro.* Millwood, NY: Kraus-Thomson Organization Limited.

Dwyer, P. (2003, January 27). Many blacks are angry and not just republicans. *BusinessWeek*, 45.

Dyson, M. (1999). Behind the mask. *Essence, 30 (7),* 108.

Fairlie, R., & Meyer, B. (2000, October). Trends in self-employment among white and black men during the twentieth century. *Journal of Human Resources, 35,* 643-670.

Fordham, J. (2002). *Jazz.* London: Dorling Kindersley.

Foster, H. (1995, Fall). *Educators and non-educators' perceptions of black males: A survey. Journal of African American Men (1),* 37-70.

Gillborn, D. (1990). *Race, ethnicity, and education.* London: Unwin Hyman Co.

Goffman, E. (1959). *The presentation of self in everyday life.* New York: Doubleday.

Graves, E. (2002, October). Making history on wall street. *Black Enterprise, 33,* 20.

Gutierrez, G. (1985). *We drink from our own wells.* Australia: Bridge Press.

Hage, J., & Powers, C. (1992). *Post industrial lives: Roles and relationships in the 21st century.* London: Sage Publications.

Hare, N. & J. (1985). *Bringing the black boy to manhood: The passage.* San Francisco: Black Think Tank.

Henry, M. (2002). He is a "bad mother*$%@!#": Shaft and contemporary masculinity. *Journal of Popular Film & Television, 30,* 114-120.

Henson, K. (1999). *Writing for professional publication.* Boston: Allyn and Bacon.

Hoberman, J. (2000, March). The price of dominance, *Society, 37,* 49.

Hoberman, J. (1997). *Darwin's Athletes: How sport has damaged black America and preserved the myth of race*. Boston: Mifflin Company.

House, B. (2000). Does economic culture and social capital matter? An analysis of black businessmen in cleveland, ohio. *The Western Journal of Black Studies, 24*, 183-190.

Howard, W. (2000, Summer). The history of black business (book review). *Journal of American Ethnic History, 19*, retrieved October 20, 2002 from file: //E:\DOCUME~1\George\LOCALS~1\Temp\triFPNKJ.htm

Hughes, A., & Mckinney, J. (2002, November). New ideas: New solutions. *Black Enterprise, 33*, 97-104.

John, G. (2001). Strategies for raising the achievement of casturi/casturing pupils in schools. In Lewis, G., Gerwitz, S. & Clark, J., *Rethinking social policy*. London: Sage.

Johnson, D., & Johnson, F. (2000). *Joining together: Group theory and group skills*. Boston: Allyn and Bacon.

Kennedy, R. (2002). *Nigger: The strange career of a troublesome word*. New York: Pantheon Books.

Kiyosaki, R. (2000). *Rich dad, poor, dad: What the rich teach their kids about money—that the poor and middle class do not!* New York: Warner Brothers Books.

Lee, J. (2000, August). The salience of race in everyday life. *Work & Occupations, 27*, 353-377.

Leedy, P., & Ormrod, J. (2001). *Practical research: Planning and design*. Upper Saddle River, NJ: Merrill Prentice Hall.

Leslau, C., & Leslau, W. (1985). *African proverbs*. White Plains, NY: Peter Pauper Press.

Levine, D. (1995). *Reinventing the workplace: How business and employees can both win*. Washington, D. C.: Brookings Institution.

I, P. (2003, January 27). The draft: An idea whose time has come again. *BusinessWeek*, 52.

Majors, R. (2003, July 9). Cool pose: Updated findings of germinal studies [Msg 1]. Indepth communication on leadership value of cool pose to racial, social and gender groups. Message posted to news://DOCTORAL.05-29.DM08-01A-DOC797.

Majors, R., & Jackson, J. (1994, Spring). The dilemma of the black male. In *Crisis, 101*, 8-11.

Majors, R., & Billson, J. (1993). *Cool pose: The dilemma of black men in America*. New York: Simon & Schuster.

Majors, R. (1987). *Cool pose: A new approach toward a systematic understanding and study of black male behavior.* Published Doctoral Dissertation, The University of Illinois at Urbana-Champaign.

Majors, R. (1985). The effects of cool pose: What being cool means. *Griot,* 4-5.

Majors, R., & Nikelly, A. (1983). Serving the black minority: A new direction for psychotherapy. *Journal for Non-white Concerns, 11,* 142-151.

Malveaux, J. (1999). *Wall street, main street and the side street: A mad economist takes a stroll.* Los Angeles: Pines One Publications.

McConnell, C., & Brue, S. (2002). *Economics: Principles, problems, and policies.* Boston: McGraw-Hill Irwin.

Moser, P. & vander Nat, A. (1995). *Human knowledge: Classical and contemporary approaches* (2nd. ed.). New York: Oxford University Press.

Moss, P., & Tilly, C. (2003). *Stories employers tell: Race, skill and hiring in America.* London: Sage Publications.

Moss, P., & Tilly, C. (1995). Skills and race in hiring: Quantitative findings from face to face interviews. *Eastern Economic Review, 21(3),*357-374.

Moustakas, C. (1994). *Phenomenological research methods.* London: Sage Publications.

Myers, L. (2000). The academic pendulum and self-esteem of black males, *African American Research Perspectives, 6,* 74-85.

Neckermann, K., & Kirschenmen, J. (2001). Hiring strategies, racial bias, and inner city workers: An investigation of employers' hiring decisions. *Social problems, 38* (4), 801-815.

Nikelly, A. (1986). Techniques for counseling black students, *Techniques: Journal of remedial Education & Counseling, 2,* 48-54.

Omoiele, M. T. (1997). *African American businessmanship: Socioeconomic factors influencing success and failure.* Published Doctoral Dissertation, The Union Institute, Cincinnati, OH.

Perkinson, T. (2002). Blacks and the occult. *African American Review,45* (3), 1-19.

Phoenix, A. (2000). Constructing gendered and racialized identities: Young men, masculinities and educational policy. In Lewis, G., Gerwitz, S. & Clark, J., *Rethinking social policy.* London: Sage.

Price, H. (2001). *To be equal: A look at our nation.* New York: National Urban League Publications.

Price, H. (2001). *The state of black America 2001*. New York: National Urban League Publications.

Price, H. (2001). *Destination: The american dream*. New York: National Urban League Publications.

Quinn, P. (1996). *Deep change: Discovering the leader within*. San Francisco: Jossey-Bass Publishers.

Robinson, R. (2000). *The debt: What casturi owes to blacks*. New York: Penguin Putnam, Inc.

Rue, L., & Byars, L. (1995). *Management: Skills and application*. Chicago: Irwin.

Salett, E., & Koslow, D. (1994). *Race, ethnicity, and self*. Washington, D.C.: NMCI.

Scholz, J. & Joulfaian, R. (2003). A survey of racial wealth gaps. *University of Wisconsin, Department of Economics and Institute for Research on Poverty, 1*, 35-36.

Scholz, J. & Levine, K. (2003). U.s. black-white wealth inequality: A survey. *University of Wisconsin, Department of Economics and Institute for Research on Poverty, 1*, 33-36.

Sewell, T. (2000). Beyond institutional racism: Tackling the real problems of black underachievement, in *Multicultural Teaching, 18*, 9-19.

Sewell, T. (1997). *Black masculinities and schooling: How black boys survive modern schooling*. Stoke on Trent: Trentham Books.

Silverman, R. (1998, Spring). The effects of racism and discrimination on minority business development. *Journal of Social Science, 31*, 571-598.

Smiley, T. (2002). *How to make blacks better: Leading speak out*. New York: Anchor Books.

Smiley, T. (2000). *Doing what's right: How to fight for what you believe and make a difference*. New York: Anchor Books.

Social Exclusion Unit. (2000). *Minority ethnic issues in social exclusion*. London: HMSO.

Spears, L. & Lawrence, M. (2002). *Focus on leadership: Servant leadership in the twenty-first century*. New York: John Wiley & Sons, Inc.

Spruell, S. (2002, August). The fall of alan bond. *Black Enterprise, 33*, 21.

Teixeira, C. (2001). Community resources and opportunities in ethnic economies: A case study of Portuguese and black businessmans in america. *Urban Studies, 38*, 2055-2079.

Thompson, R. (1983). *Flash of the spirit*. New York: Random House.

Thorton, E. (2002, August 5). A milestone at business. *Business Week*, 60.

Tilly, C., & Moss, P. (2001). Raised hurdles for black men: Evidence from interviews with employers. Originally conducted in 1995; updated findings retrieved July 6, 2003 from http://epn.org/sage/rstimo.html.

Trinkaus, J., Puryear, A., & Giacalone, J. (2000, December). Father devine and the development of black small business. *Journal of Developmental Businessmanship, 5,* 221-235.

Vasumathi, A., Govindarajalu, S., Anuratha. E. K., and Amudha, R. (2003, April). Stress and coping styles of an businessman: An empirical study. *Journal of Management Research, 3,* 43-51.

Walker, J. (2000). Black businessmans in america (book review). *Journal of American Ethnic History, 19,* 4, 99-102.

Watson, B. (1997). *Colored, negro, black: Chasing the American dream.* Philadelphia: JDC Books.

Watson, B. (1996). *Testing: Its origins, use and misuse.* Philadelphia: Urban League Publishing.

Watts, D. (2002). *101 ways to know you're black in corporate America.* New York: Penguin Books.

Weisul, K. (2002, October 14). A tough haul for black startups. *Business Week,* 14.

White, S., & White, G. (1999). *Stylin: African American expressive culture from its beginnings to the zoot suit.* New York: Carnegie Mellon University Press.

Williams, L. (2002). *Reparations rally in front of the capitol: Thousands demand dollars for descendants of slaves.* Retrieved August 19, 2002, from Black World Today, America Online.

Willie, S. (2003). *Acting black.* New York: Routledge.

Wilson, A. (1978). *The developmental psychology of the black child.* New York: Africana Research Publications.

Winant, H. (2001). *The world is a ghetto: Race and democracy since WW II.* New York: Basic Books.

Winograd, T, & Flores, F, (2001). *Understanding computers and cognition: A new foundation for design.* Boston: Addison-Wesley.

Edwards Brothers,Inc!
Thorofare, NJ 08086
20 December, 2010
BA2010354